DRAMA STUDY GUIDE

The Tragedy of Othello

BY WILLIAM SHAKESPEARE

HOLT, RINEHART AND WINSTON

Harcourt Brace & Company

Austin · New York · Orlando · Atlanta · San Francisco · Boston · Dallas · Toronto · London

Teachers using *Drama Study Guide: The Tragedy of Othello* may photocopy
complete pages in sufficient quantities for classroom use only and not for resale.

Cover art: Joe Melomo, Design Director; Shoehorn, Inc., Designer; Andrew Yates,
Photographer; Mike Gobbi, Photo Researcher

HRW is a registered trademark licensed to Holt, Rinehart and Winston.

Printed in the United States of America

ISBN 0-03-057317-3

2 3 4 5 6 054 04 03 02 01

Contents

INTRODUCTION

Holt, Rinehart and Winston's *Drama Study Guides* offer you and your students a rich fund of information for understanding, interpreting, and appreciating a variety of plays commonly taught in the classroom. Teachers, whether they are intimately familiar with the play or have never before taught it—perhaps not even read it—will find the Study Guide an informative, creative, and time-saving resource. Students will find that the material in each Study Guide greatly enriches their experience of the play. The Study Guide will help them respond to the play, aid their literal comprehension, deepen their interpretations of the play, increase their ability to recognize and respond to literary elements, stimulate their creative responses to literature, and provide them with opportunities to exercise their critical thinking skills and their writing abilities.

Each *Drama Study Guide* is designed to allow you to teach the play in the way that seems best for your students and most comfortable for you. Many sections of the Study Guide can be duplicated and then distributed to your students, either as the entire class reads a play together or as individual students or small groups of students study a particular play on their own. The materials in the Study Guide are not intended to lead to one prescribed interpretation of the play but to act as a catalyst for discussions, analyses, interpretations, conclusions, and further research.

The following are descriptions of the major sections of this Study Guide.

Focusing on Background

Before they can fully appreciate any play, most students need some relevant background information. This section therefore supplies important information about the author's life, along with a brief discussion of his other works and philosophical orientation and comments on the play's historical context and theatrical history. For Shakespeare's plays the teacher is reminded of the rich background material already available in the *Elements of Literature* Pupil's and Annotated Teacher's Editions.

Critical Responses to the Play

An essay on critics' responses to the play includes short excerpts of analyses written by Shakespearean scholars and puts this criticism in a historical context. It provides interpretations of aspects of the play. Students may use this commentary as a starting point for their own interpretive essays.

Elements of the Play

This section of the Study Guide first presents an outline of the key literary elements and an overview of the key themes, which should be valuable to you in determining how you want to present the play to your class. It is followed by the play's cast of characters, an annotated list that comprises summaries of the characters' roles in the plot and their relationships to one another. Next is a more detailed analysis of important elements of the play—the setting, the structure, and the language.

Some of the material in this section may be shared with students as they read the play; some will be valuable after they have read it. If students need a quick review of the definitions of literary elements, refer them to the Handbook of Literary Terms at the back of the *Elements of Literature* Pupil's Editions.

Teaching the Play

In this section are suggestions to help you set Objectives for the study of the play, introduce the drama to your class, and read the play with your entire class and with individual students. Here you will also find a section called Options for Teaching the Play, which will give you many, many practical and creative ideas for varying your instructional methods to suit the needs of particular students and particular classes.

Plot Synopsis and Literary Focus

This section presents an act-by-act summary of the action and the literary focus of the play. It is particularly useful as a timesaver and is helpful if you are teaching the play for the first time. You will probably not wish to duplicate this material for your students because they might read it instead of the play itself. You may, however, choose to share the material with students for review, reteaching, or enrichment after they have read and fully discussed the play in class.

Guided Reading

Focusing on staging, characterization, plot development, and interpretation of action and dialogue, the questions in this section are designed to help you help students interpret the play *as they read it*. Questions correspond to specific lines in the play, and an answer or a suggested answer immediately follows each question. You may want to use these questions with students who are having difficulty with the play, giving them opportunities to follow plot and character development. Some students may find these questions useful springboards for research projects or

*Drama Study Guide: **The Tragedy of Othello, the Moor of Venice***

writing assignments. If students perform parts of the play, some of these questions will help them think as directors or actors.

The following tools for instruction and assessment are provided for each act of the play or for the play as a whole. This material is presented in the form of worksheets, questions, and activities, all of which may be duplicated for students' use.

The exercises in the **Graphic Organizer for Active Reading** give students the opportunity to record responses and organize their ideas before and/or after they read each act of the play.

Making Meanings opens with literal recall questions (Reviewing the Text) and then moves on to questions calling for higher-level thinking skills, including responding to the text, inferential thinking, generalizing, predicting, extending the text, and even challenging the text. Following Act V are Making Meanings questions for the play as a whole. These require students to make informed judgments about the play by drawing on their skills of analysis, synthesis, and evaluation.

Making Meanings questions are designed for maximum flexibility. These questions, which are provided for each act of the play, may be distributed to students prior to their reading of an act so that they can read it with more focus. The questions may also be used for classroom discussion. Alternatively, they may be answered in writing as homework or as an in-class assignment.

Students should be encouraged to respond to at least some of the Making Meanings questions in writing even if you use these questions primarily as a basis for classroom discussion. Students may then record their answers in a journal or a reading log—a notebook of creative, critical, and emotional responses that they record as they read the text. Students may share, and use interactively, material from these notebooks with one another and/or with you.

Words to Own Worksheets consist of exercises using words from the play.

Literary Elements Worksheets identify key literary elements in the play. Each worksheet contains exercises that test students' recognition and understanding of these elements.

Tests, reproducible for classroom use, include objective questions that are based on recall of key events in the plot, questions that require an analysis of literary elements, and short essay questions that cover the interpretation, evaluation, and analysis of the play.

There is also a **Test** for the play as a whole and one for **Testing the Genre.**

Choices: Building Your Portfolio, provided for the play as a whole, is a collection of critical and creative assignments that call for writing, research, performance, and artwork. Creative writing assignments extend the play to new territory. For example, an assignment may ask students to retell an important episode or rewrite the ending of the play in their own words. It may ask them to write an imagined sequel to the play or to cast appropriate contemporary actors in the roles of the play's main characters. All these assignments enable students to demonstrate creatively their understanding of the play. Critical writing assignments ask students to respond to the play through a critical-analytical route. For example, an assignment may ask students to respond to a critic's comments about the play, supporting or refuting those comments using specific evidence from the play. It may ask them to compare and contrast two characters in the play or to demonstrate how a theme of the play is captured in a recurring symbol.

Choices activities also suggest research projects and assignments in drama, art, and music that take the student beyond the play itself and allow you to make valuable cross-curriculum connections.

Language Link Worksheet   This worksheet offers a hands-on approach to an understanding of English as it was used in Shakespeare's day and to an appreciation of the poetic conventions that Shakespeare employed.

Cross-Curricular Activity   This interdisciplinary, theme-based activity is appropriate for team teaching.

Read On   This section is included for teachers and students who wish to extend their reading. It lists works by other writers that use topics or themes connected with the play.

Answer Key   The Answer Key is complete, providing answers to objective questions as well as to interpretive questions, to which there is no one correct answer. In the latter case, several possible responses may be suggested.

Focusing on Background

The Life and Work of William Shakespeare (1564–1616)

by **C. F. Main**   C. F. Main was for many years a professor of English at Rutgers University in New Brunswick, New Jersey. He is the editor of *Poems: Wadsworth Handbook and Anthology* and has written reviews and articles on sixteenth-, seventeenth-, and eighteenth-century literature.

Every literate person has heard of William Shakespeare, the author of more than three dozen remarkable plays and more than 150 poems. Over the centuries these literary works have made such a deep impression on the human race that all sorts of fancies, legends, and theories have been invented about their author. There are even those who say that somebody other than Shakespeare wrote the works that bear his name, although these deluded people cannot agree on who, among a dozen candidates, this other author actually was. Such speculation is based on the wrong assumption that little is known about Shakespeare's life; in fact, Shakespeare's life is better documented than the life of any other dramatist of the time except perhaps Ben Jonson, a writer who seems almost modern in the way he publicized himself. Jonson was an honest, blunt, and outspoken man who knew Shakespeare well; for a time the two dramatists wrote for the same theatrical company, and Shakespeare even acted in Jonson's plays. Often ungenerous in his praise of other writers, Jonson published a poem asserting that Shakespeare was superior to all Greek, Roman, and other English dramatists and predicting that he would be "not of an age, but for all time." Jonson's judgment is now commonly accepted, and his prophecy has come true.

Shakespeare was born in Stratford-on-Avon, a historic and prosperous market town in Warwickshire, and was christened in the parish church there on April 26, 1564. His father was John Shakespeare, a merchant at one time active in the town government; his mother—born Mary Arden—came from a prominent family in the country. For seven years or so William attended the Stratford Grammar School, where he obtained an excellent education in Latin, the Bible, and English composition. (The students had to write out English translations of Latin works and then turn them back into Latin.) After leaving school, he may have been apprenticed to a butcher, but because he shows in his plays very detailed knowledge of many different crafts and trades, scholars have proposed a number of different occupations that he could have followed. At eighteen, Shakespeare married Anne Hathaway, the twenty-seven-year-old daughter of a farmer living near Stratford. They had three children, a daughter named Susanna and twins named Hamnet and Judith. We don't know how the young Shakespeare supported his family, but according to tradition he taught school for a few years. The two daughters grew up and married; the son died when he was eleven.

How did Shakespeare first become interested in the theater? Presumably by seeing plays. We know that traveling acting companies frequently visited Stratford, and we assume that he attended their performances and that he also went to the nearby city of Coventry, where a famous cycle of religious plays was put on every year. But to be a dramatist, one had to be in London, where the theater was flourishing in the 1580s. Just when Shakespeare left his family and moved to London (there is no evidence that his wife was ever in the city) is uncertain; scholars say that he arrived there in 1587 or 1588. It is certain that he was busy and successful in the London theater by 1592, when a fellow dramatist named Robert Greene attacked him in print and ridiculed a passage in his early play *Henry VI*. Greene, a down-and-out Cambridge graduate, warned other university men then writing plays to beware of this "upstart crow beautified with our feathers." Greene died of dissipation just as his ill-natured attack was being published, but a friend of his named Henry Chettle immediately apologized in print to Shakespeare and commended Shakespeare's acting and writing ability, and his personal honesty.

From 1592 on, there is ample documentation of Shakespeare's life and works. We know where he lived in London, at least approximately when his plays were produced and printed, and even how he spent his money. From 1594 to his retirement in about 1613, he was continuously a member of one company, which also included the great tragic actor Richard Burbage and the popular clown Will Kemp. Although actors and others connected with the theater had a very low status legally, in practice they enjoyed the patronage of noblemen and even royalty. It is a mistake to think of Shakespeare as an obscure actor who somehow wrote great

*Drama Study Guide: **The Tragedy of Othello, the Moor of Venice***

HRW MATERIAL COPYRIGHTED UNDER NOTICE APPEARING EARLIER IN THIS WORK.

3

plays; he was well-known even as a young man. He first became famous as the author of a best-seller, an erotic narrative poem called *Venus and Adonis* (1593). This poem, as well as a more serious one entitled *Lucrece* (1594), was dedicated to a rich and extravagant young nobleman, the earl of Southampton. The dedication of *Lucrece* suggests that Shakespeare and his patron were on very friendly terms.

Shakespeare's Early Plays

Among Shakespeare's earliest plays are the following, with the generally but not universally accepted dates of their first performance: *Richard III* (1592–1593), a "chronicle," or history, about a deformed usurper who became king of England; *The Comedy of Errors* (1592–1593), a rowdy farce of mistaken identity based on a Latin play; *Titus Andronicus* (1593–1594), a blood-and-thunder tragedy full of rant and atrocities; *The Taming of the Shrew* (1593–1594), *The Two Gentlemen of Verona* (1593–1595), and *Love's Labor's Lost* (1593–1594), three agreeable comedies; and *Romeo and Juliet* (1594–1595), a poetic tragedy of ill-fated lovers. The extraordinary thing about these plays is not so much their immense variety—each one is quite different from all the others—but the fact that they are all regularly revived and performed on stages all over the world today.

By 1596, Shakespeare was beginning to prosper. He had his father apply to the Heralds' College for a coat of arms that the family could display, signifying that they were "gentlefolks." On Shakespeare's family crest a falcon is shown, shaking a spear. To support this claim to gentility, Shakespeare bought New Place, a handsome house and grounds in Stratford, a place so commodious and elegant that the queen of England once stayed there after Shakespeare's daughter Susanna inherited it. Shakespeare also, in 1599, joined with a few other members of his company, now called the Lord Chamberlain's Men, to finance a new theater on the south side of the Thames—the famous Globe. The "honey-tongued Shakespeare," as he was called in a book about English literature published in 1598, was now earning money as a playwright, an actor, and a shareholder in a theater. By 1600, Shakespeare was regularly associating with members of the aristocracy, and six of his plays had been given command performances at the court of Queen Elizabeth.

During the last years of Elizabeth I's reign, Shakespeare completed his cycle of plays about England during the Wars of the Roses: *Richard II* (1595–1596), both parts of *Henry IV* (1597–1598), and *Henry V* (1599–1600). Also in this period he wrote the play most frequently studied in schools—*Julius Caesar* (1599–1600)—and the comedies that are most frequently performed today: *A Midsummer Night's Dream* (1595–1596), *The Merchant of Venice* (1596–1597), *Much Ado About Nothing* (1598–1599), and *As You Like It* and *Twelfth Night* (1599–1600). And finally at this time he wrote or rewrote *Hamlet* (1600–1601), the tragedy that, of all his tragedies, has provoked the most varied and controversial interpretations from critics, scholars, and actors.

Shakespeare indeed prospered under Queen Elizabeth; according to an old tradition, she asked him to write *The Merry Wives of Windsor* (1600–1601) because she wanted to see the merry, fat old knight Sir John Falstaff (of the *Henry* plays) in love.

He prospered even more under Elizabeth's successor, King James of Scotland. Fortunately for Shakespeare's company, as it turned out, James's royal entry into London in 1603 had to be postponed for several months because the plague was raging in the city. While waiting for the epidemic to subside, the royal court stayed in various palaces outside London. Shakespeare's company took advantage of this situation and, since the city theaters were closed, performed several plays for the court and the new king. Shakespeare's plays delighted James, for he loved literature and was starved for pleasure after the grim experience of ruling Scotland for many years. He immediately took the company under his patronage, renamed it the King's Men, gave its members patents to perform anywhere in the realm, provided them with special clothing for state occasions, increased their salaries, and appointed their chief members, including Shakespeare, to be grooms of the Royal Chamber. All this patronage brought such prosperity to Shakespeare that he was able to make some very profitable real estate investments in Stratford and London.

Shakespeare's "Tragic Period"

In the early years of the seventeenth century, while his financial affairs were flourishing and everything was apparently going very well for Shakespeare, he wrote his greatest tragedies: *Hamlet* (already mentioned), *Othello* (1604–1605), *King Lear* (1605–1606), *Macbeth* (1605–1606), and *Antony and Cleopatra* (1606–1607). Because these famous plays are so preoccupied with evil, violence, and death, some people feel that Shakespeare must have been very unhappy and depressed when he wrote them. Moreover, such people find even the comedies he wrote at this time more sour than sweet: *Troilus and Cressida* (1601–1603), *All's Well That*

*Drama Study Guide: **The Tragedy of Othello, the Moor of Venice***

Ends Well (1602–1603), and *Measure for Measure* (1604–1605). And so, instead of paying tribute to Shakespeare's powerful imagination, which is everywhere evident, these people invent a "tragic period" in Shakespeare's biography, and they search for personal crises in his private life. When they cannot find these agonies, they invent them. To be sure, in 1607 an actor named Edward Shakespeare, who may well have been William's younger brother, died in London. But by 1607 Shakespeare's alleged "tragic period" was almost over!

It is quite wrong to assume a one-to-one correspondence between writers' lives and their works, because writers must be allowed to imagine whatever they can. It is especially wrong in the case of a writer like Shakespeare, who did not write to express himself but to satisfy the patrons of the theater that he and his partners owned. Shakespeare must have repeatedly given the audience just what it wanted; otherwise, he could not have made so much money out of the theater. To insist that he had to experience and feel personally everything that he wrote about is absurd. He wrote about King Lear, who cursed his two monstrous daughters for treating him very badly; in contrast, what evidence there is suggests that he got along very well with his own two daughters. And so, instead of "tragic," we should think of the years 1600–1607 as glorious, because in them Shakespeare's productivity was at its peak. It seems very doubtful that a depressed person would write plays like these. In fact, they would make their creator feel exhilarated rather than sad.

The Last Years

In 1612, Shakespeare decided that, having made a considerable sum from his plays and theatrical enterprises, he would retire to his handsome house in Stratford, a place he had never forgotten, though he seems to have kept his life there rather separate from his life in London. His retirement was not complete, for the records show that after he returned to Stratford, he still took part in the management of the King's Men and their two theaters: the Globe, a polygonal building opened in 1599 and used for performances in good weather, and the Blackfriars, acquired in 1608 and used for indoor performances. Shakespeare's works in this period show no signs of diminished creativity, except that in some years he wrote one play instead of the customary two, and they continue to illustrate the great diversity of his genius. Among them are the tragedies *Timon of Athens* (1607–1608) and *Coriolanus* (1607–1608) and five plays that have been variously classified as comedies, romances, or tragicomedies: *Pericles* (1608–1609), *Cymbeline* (1609–1610), *The Winter's Tale* (1610–1611),

The Tempest (1611–1612), and *The Two Noble Kinsmen* (1612–1613). His last English history play, *Henry VIII* (1612–1613), contains a tribute to Queen Elizabeth—a somewhat tardy tribute, because, unlike most of the other poets of the day, Shakespeare did not praise her in print when she died in 1603. (Some scholars argue, on very little evidence, that he was an admirer of the earl of Essex, a former intimate of Elizabeth's whom she had beheaded for rebelliousness.) During the first performance of *Henry VIII,* in June of 1613, the firing of the cannon at the end of Act I set the Globe on fire (it had a thatched roof), and it burned to the ground. Only one casualty is recorded: A bottle of ale had to be poured on a man whose breeches were burning. Fortunately, the company had the Blackfriars in which to perform until the Globe could be rebuilt and reopened in 1614.

Shakespeare's last recorded visit to London, accompanied by his son-in-law Dr. John Hall, was in November 1614, though he may have gone down to the city afterward because he continued to own property there, including a building very near the Blackfriars Theater. Probably, though, he spent most of the last two years of his life at New Place, with his daughter Susanna Hall (and his granddaughter Elizabeth) living nearby. He died on April 23, 1616, and was buried under the floor of Stratford Church, with this epitaph warning posterity not to dig him up and transfer him to the graveyard outside the church—a common practice in those days when space was needed:

> Good friend, for Jesus' sake forbear
> To dig the bones enclosèd here!
> Blest be the man that spares these stones,
> And curst be he that moves my bones.

Shakespeare's Genius

What sort of man was Shakespeare? This is a very hard question to answer because he left no letters, diaries, or other private writings containing his personal views; instead, he left us plays, and in a good play the actors do not speak for the dramatist but for the characters they are impersonating. We cannot, then, say that Shakespeare approved of evil because he created murderers or advocated religion because he created clergymen; we cannot say that he believed in fatalism because he created fatalists or admired flattery because he created flatterers. All these would be naive, and contradictory, reactions to the plays. Shakespeare's characters represent such a vast range of human behavior and attitudes that they must be products of his careful observation and fertile imagination rather than extensions of himself. A critic named Desmond McCarthy once

*Drama Study Guide: **The Tragedy of Othello, the Moor of Venice***

HRW MATERIAL COPYRIGHTED UNDER NOTICE APPEARING EARLIER IN THIS WORK.

5

said that trying to identify Shakespeare the man in his plays is like looking at a very dim portrait under glass: The more you peer at it, the more you see only yourself.

One thing is certain: Shakespeare was a complete man of the theater who created works specifically for his own acting company and his own stage. He had, for instance, to provide good parts in every play for the principal performers in the company, including the comedians acting in tragedies. Since there were no actresses, he had to limit the number of female parts in his plays and create them in such a way that they could readily be taken by boys. For instance, although there are many fathers in the plays, there are very few mothers: While boys could be taught to flirt and play shy, acting maternally would be difficult for them. Several of Shakespeare's young women disguise themselves as young men early in Act I—an easy solution to the problem of boys playing girls' parts. Shakespeare also had to provide the words for songs because theatergoers expected singing in every play; furthermore, the songs had to be devised so that they would exhibit the talents of particular actors with good voices. Since many of the plays contain many characters, and since there were a limited number of actors in the company, Shakespeare had to arrange for doubling and even tripling of roles; that is, a single actor would have to perform more than one part. Since, of course, an actor could impersonate only one character at a time, Shakespeare had to plan his scenes carefully so that nobody would ever have to be onstage in two different roles at the same time. A careful study of the plays shows that Shakespeare handled all these technical problems of dramaturgy very masterfully.

Although the plays are primarily performance scripts, from earliest times the public has wanted to read them as well as see them staged. In every generation, people have felt that the plays contain so much wisdom, so much knowledge of human nature, so much remarkable poetry, that they need to be pondered in private as well as enjoyed in public. Most readers have agreed with what the poet John Dryden said about Shakespeare's "soul": The man who wrote the plays may be elusive, but he was obviously a great genius whose lofty imagination is matched by his sympathy for all kinds of human behavior. Reading the plays, then, is a rewarding experience in itself; it is also excellent preparation for seeing them performed onstage or on film.

Shakespeare's contemporaries were so eager to read his plays that enterprising publishers did everything possible, including stealing them, to make them available. Of course the company generally tried to keep the plays unpublished because they did not want them performed by rival companies. Even so, eighteen plays were published in small books, called quartos, before Shakespeare's partners collected them and published them after his death. This collection, known as the first folio because of its large size, was published in 1623. Surviving copies of this folio are regarded as valuable treasures today. But, of course, the general reader need not consult any of the original texts of Shakespeare because his works never go out of print; they are always available in many different languages and many different formats. The plays that exist in two different versions (one in a quarto and one in the folio) have provided scholars with endless matter for speculation about what Shakespeare actually intended the correct text to be. Indeed, every aspect of Shakespeare has been, and continues to be, thoroughly studied and written about, by literary and historical scholars, by theater and film people, by experts in many fields, and by amateurs of every stripe. No wonder that he is mistakenly regarded as a great mystery.

The Renaissance Theater

by **C. F. Main**

By the mid-sixteenth century, the art of drama in England was three centuries old, but the idea of housing it in a permanent building was new, and even after theaters had been built, plays were still regularly performed in improvised spaces when acting companies were touring the provinces or presenting their plays in the large houses of royalty and nobility.

In 1576, James Burbage, the father of Shakespeare's partner and fellow actor Richard Burbage, built the first public theater and called it, appropriately, the Theater. Shortly thereafter, a second playhouse, called the Curtain, was erected. Both of these were located in a northern suburb of London, where they would not affront the more staid and sober-minded residents of London proper. Then came the Rose, the Swan, the Fortune, the Globe, the Red Bull, and the Hope: an astonishing number of public theaters and far more than there were in any other capital city of Europe at that time.

*Drama Study Guide: **The Tragedy of Othello, the Moor of Venice***

The Globe

The Globe, of course, is the most famous of these because it was owned by the company that Shakespeare belonged to. It was built out of timbers salvaged from the Theater when the latter was demolished in 1599. These timbers were carted across London, rafted over the Thames, and reassembled on the Bankside near a beer garden—not the most elegant of London suburbs. Since many of Shakespeare's plays received their first performances in the Globe, curiosity and speculation about this famous building have been common for the last two hundred years or more. Unfortunately, the plans for the Globe have not survived, though there still exist old panoramic drawings of London in which its exterior is pictured, and there is still considerable information available about some other theaters, including a sketch of the Swan's stage and the building contract for the Fortune. But the most important sources of information are the plays themselves, with their stage directions and other clues to the structure of the theater.

The Structure of the Globe

At the present time most scholars accept as accurate the reconstruction of the Globe published by the contemporary British author C. Walter Hodges. The theater had three main parts: the building proper, the stage, and the tiring house (or backstage area), with a flag that flew from its peak whenever there was to be a performance that day.

The theater building proper was a wooden structure three stories high surrounding a spacious inner yard open to the sky. It was probably a sixteen-sided polygon. Any structure with that many sides would appear circular, so it is not surprising that Shakespeare referred to the Globe as "the wooden O" in his play *Henry V*. There were probably only two entrances to the building, one for the public and one for the theater company, but there may well have been another public door used as an exit, because when the Globe burned down in 1613, the crowd escaped the flames quickly and safely. General admission to the theater cost one penny; this entitled a spectator to be a groundling, which meant he or she could stand in the yard. Patrons paid a little more to mount up into the galleries, where there were seats and where there was a better view of the stage, along its two sides; people who wanted to be conspicuous rented them, and they must have been a great nuisance to the rest of the audience and the actors. A public theater could hold a surprisingly large number of spectators: three thousand, according to two different contemporary accounts. The spectators must

have been squeezed together, and so it is no wonder that the authorities always closed the theaters during epidemics of plague. The stage jutted halfway out into the yard so that the actors were in much closer contact with the audience than they are in modern theaters, most of which have picture-frame stages with orchestra pit, proscenium arch, and front curtains. A picture-frame stage usually attempts to give the illusion of reality: Its painted scenery represents the walls of a room or an outdoor vista, and the actors pretend that nobody is watching them perform, at least until it is time to take a bow. To be sure, theater designs have been changing since World War II, and people have again learned to enjoy plays "in the round," without elaborate realistic settings. Modern audiences are learning to accept what Renaissance audiences took for granted: that the theater cannot show reality. Whatever happens on the stage is make-believe. Spectators at the Globe loved to see witches or devils emerge through the trapdoor in the stage, which everybody pretended led down to hell, though everybody knew that it did not, just as everybody knew that the ceiling over part of the stage was not really the heavens. This ceiling was painted with elaborate suns, moons, and stars, and it contained a trapdoor through which angels, gods, and spirits could be lowered on a wire and even flown over the other actors' heads. Such large sensational effects as these were plentiful in the Renaissance theater. At the opposite extreme, every tiny nuance of an individual actor's performance could affect the audience, which was also very close to the stage. The actors were highly trained, and they could sing, dance, declaim, wrestle, fence, clown, roar, weep, and whisper. Unfortunately, none of this liveliness can be conveyed by the printed page; we must imagine all the activity onstage as we read.

The third structural element in this theater was the tiring house, a tall building that contained machinery and dressing rooms and that provided a two-story back wall for the stage. Hodges's drawing shows that this wall contained a gallery above and a curtained space below. The gallery had multiple purposes, depending on what play was being performed. Spectators could sit there, musicians could perform there, or parts of the play could be acted there. Many plays have stage directions indicating that some actors should appear on a level above the other actors—on the balconies, towers, city walls, parapets, fortifications, hills, and the like. The curtained area below the gallery was used mainly for "discoveries" of things prepared in advance and temporarily kept hidden from the audience until the proper time for showing them. In Shakespeare's *Merchant of Venice,* for example, the curtain is drawn to reveal (or "discover") three small chests, in one of which is hidden the heroine's picture. Some modern accounts of Renaissance theaters refer to this curtained area as an inner stage, but apparently it was too small, too shallow, and too far out of the sight of some spectators to be used as a performance space. If a performer was "discovered" behind the curtains, as Marlowe's Dr. Faustus is discovered in his study with his books, he would quickly move out onto the stage to be better seen and heard. Thrones, banquets, beds, writing desks, and so on could be pushed through the curtains onto the stage, and as soon as a large property of this sort appeared, the audience would know at once that the action was taking place indoors. When the action shifted to the outdoors, the property could be pulled back behind the curtain.

Scenery

The people in the audience were quite prepared to use their imaginations. When they saw actors carrying lanterns, they knew it was night even though the sun was shining brightly overhead. Often, instead of seeing a scene, they heard it described, as when a character exclaims,

> But look, the morn in russet mantle clad,
> Walks o'er the dew of yon high eastward hill.
> —*Hamlet,*
> Act I, Scene 1

Shakespeare could not show a sunrise; instead of trying to, he wrote a speech inviting the audience to imagine one. When the stage had to become a forest, as in several of Shakespeare's comedies, there was no painted scenery trying (and usually failing) to look like real trees, bushes, flowers, and so on. Instead, a few bushes and small trees might be pushed onto the stage, and then the actors created the rest of the scenery by speaking poetry that evoked images in the spectators' minds. In *As You Like It,* Rosalind simply looks around her and announces "Well, this is the Forest of Arden."

The great advantage of this theater was its speed and flexibility. The stage could be anywhere, and the play did not have to be interrupted while the sets were shifted. By listening to what was being said, members of the audience learned all that they needed to know about where the action was taking place at any given moment; they did not need to consult a printed program.

Act and Scene Divisions

Most of the act and scene divisions in Renaissance drama have been added by later editors, who have tried to adapt plays written for the old platform stage

to the modern picture-frame stage. In this process, editors have badly damaged one play in particular, Shakespeare's *Antony and Cleopatra.* This play was published and republished for a hundred years after Shakespeare's death without any act and scene divisions at all. Then one editor cut it up into twenty-seven different scenes, and another into forty-four, thus better suiting the play to the picture-frame stage, or so they thought. But a stage manager would go mad trying to provide realistic scenery for this many different locales. Even a reader becomes confused and irritated trying to imagine all the different places where the characters are going according to the modern stage directions, which are of a kind that Shakespeare and his contemporaries never heard of. "Theirs was a drama of persons, not a drama of places," according to Gerald Bentley, one of our best theatrical historians.

Props and Effects

Some modern accounts have overemphasized the bareness of Renaissance theaters; actually they were ornate rather than bare. Their interiors were painted brightly, there were many decorations, and the space at the rear of the stage could be covered with colorful tapestries or hangings. Costumes were rich, elaborate, and expensive. The manager-producer Philip Henslowe, whose account books preserve much important information about the early theater, once paid twenty pounds, then an enormous sum, for a single cloak for one of his actors to wear in a play. Henslowe's lists of theatrical properties mention, among other things, chariots, fountains, dragons, beds, tents, thrones, booths, wayside crosses. The audience enjoyed the processions—religious, royal, military—that occur in many plays. These would enter the stage from one door, pass over the stage, and then exit by the other door. A few quick costume changes in the tiring house, as the actors passed through, could double and triple the number of people in a procession. Pageantry, sound effects, music both vocal and instrumental—all these elements helped give members of the audience their money's worth of theatrical experience.

Private Halls and Indoor Theaters

These, then, were the chief features of the public theaters that Renaissance dramatists had to keep in mind as they wrote their plays. In addition to these theaters, the acting companies also performed in two other kinds of spaces: in the great halls of castles and manor houses and in certain indoor theaters in London (which are called indoor theaters to distinguish them from theaters like the Globe, which were only partly roofed over).

Drama Study Guide: **The Tragedy of Othello, the Moor of Venice**

For performances in a great hall, a theater company must have had a portable booth stage, a building where the usual entertainment was a bear being attacked by dogs. The bear pits were vile places, but the temporary stages set up in them could easily accommodate any play written for the public theater except for scenes requiring the use of heavens overhanging the stage.

Something like this booth stage may also have been used in the private theaters like the Blackfriars, which Shakespeare's company, the King's Men, acquired in 1608. Although nothing is known about the physical features of the Blackfriars stage, we know that the building itself—a disused monastery—was entirely roofed over, unlike the Globe, where only part of the stage and part of the audience had the protection of a roof. One great advantage of Blackfriars was that the company could perform there in cold weather and, since artificial lighting always had to be used, at night. And so the King's Men could put on plays all during the year, with increased profits for the shareholders, among them Shakespeare.

Shakespeare's Plays

Henry VI, Part II (1590–1591)
Henry VI, Part III (1590–1591)
Henry VI, Part I (1591–1592)
The Comedy of Errors (1592–1593)
Richard III (1592–1593)
Titus Andronicus (1593–1594)
The Taming of the Shrew (1593–1594)
Love's Labor's Lost (1593–1594)
The Two Gentlemen of Verona (1593–1595)
Romeo and Juliet (1594–1595)
Richard II (1595–1596)
A Midsummer Night's Dream (1595–1596)
King John (1596–1597)
The Merchant of Venice (1596–1597)
Henry IV, Part I (1597)
Henry IV, Part II (1597–1598)
Much Ado About Nothing (1598–1599)
Henry V (1599–1600)
Julius Caesar (1599–1600)

As You Like It (1599–1600)
Twelfth Night (1599–1600)
Hamlet (1600–1601)
The Merry Wives of Windsor (1600–1601)
Troilus and Cressida (1601–1603)
All's Well That Ends Well (1602–1603)
Othello (1604–1605)
Measure for Measure (1604–1605)
King Lear (1605–1606)
Macbeth (1605–1606)
Antony and Cleopatra (1606–1607)
Timon of Athens (1607–1608)
Coriolanus (1607–1608)
Pericles (1608–1609)
Cymbeline (1609–1610)
The Winter's Tale (1610–1611)
The Tempest (1611–1612)
The Two Noble Kinsmen (1612–1613)
Henry VIII (1612–1613)

Sources for *The Tragedy of Othello*

Shakespeare's principal source for *The Tragedy of Othello* was a collection of tales called *Hecatommithi* by Giraldi Cinthio, published in Venice in 1566. It is not known whether Shakespeare read these tales in the original Italian or in French or in a now lost English translation, but the similarities in plot and subject matter are too extensive to be coincidental.

Cinthio's narrative tells of a gallant Moor in the military service of Venice who falls in love with a beautiful young Venetian, Disdemona (the only named character). She loves the Moor for his virtues, not for his looks, and marries him despite her parents' opposition. When the Moor is to command the Venetian troops on Cyprus, his wife sails with him. The Moor's Ensign desires Disdemona and is consumed by jealous anger when she rejects his advances. Devious and manipulative, the seemingly upright Ensign plots his revenge against Disdemona, making use of the Moor and his close friend, the Captain, who the Ensign jealously believes has had more success with Disdemona than he has. The Ensign steals Disdemona's handkerchief and puts it in the Captain's house, then makes sure that the Moor sees the Captain leaving Disdemona when he comes to return it. Successful in turning the Moor against his wife, the Ensign manipulates him further, getting him to participate in

*Drama Study Guide: **The Tragedy of Othello, the Moor of Venice***

Disdemona's murder. Together the Ensign and the Moor fell Disdemona with a sandbag and then lower a timber roof on her so her death will look accidental. Right after the murder the Moor repents and grieves for his wife, yet he tries to escape punishment. Eventually he is killed by his wife's relatives, and the Ensign is brought to justice for another crime.

Although the similarities are obvious, the differences are equally striking. Cinthio's tale is a shallow one of sordid revenge and jealousy. His Moor, while distinguished, is hardly noble, and the audience can feel little or no sympathy for him, only pity for his innocent victim. Shakespeare, on the other hand, gives Othello great poetry to speak and a sustaining love for the woman he murders, thus bestowing on him dignity and greatness.

Although the seeds of Iago's character exist in Cinthio's Ensign, without the character of Roderigo and the device of the soliloquy, the Venetian writer fails to plumb the Ensign's hypocritical character and motives to the extent that his English successor does.

There may be a second source for *Othello:* the fourth story in Geoffrey Fenton's collection *Certain Tragical Discourses* (1567). In this tale of jealousy the suspected wife is kissed and then killed by her husband in their bedroom. The husband then, like Othello, kills himself and falls upon the body of his murdered wife.

Theatrical History of *Othello*

The first recorded performance of *Othello* took place in 1604 at Whitehall Palace and was staged for King James I (r. 1603–1625). Richard Burbage, Shakespeare's partner and fellow actor, played Othello.

The great diarist Samuel Pepys recorded seeing the play in 1660 ("a very pretty lady that sat by me, called out, to see Desdemona smothered") and again in 1669. It was in this era that actresses were first allowed to play the female roles.

Beginning in the late seventeenth century and continuing into the eighteenth, actors in the neo-classical style, like Thomas Betterton and James Quin, emphasized the dignity and nobility of the Moor. Quin, using cork to blacken his skin, played the part in the uniform of a British general. Quin's contemporary and rival, David Garrick, criticized Quin's performance as wooden and passionless. Garrick countered with an interpretation of the role that emphasized Othello's so-called barbarian origins and his descent into jealous rage. Garrick, in turn, was faulted for failing to give Othello heroic stature. (Part of the problem was Garrick's height—he wore a high turban to make himself look taller.)

The next generation of great Othellos continued to veer between the poles of dignity and passion, with John Philip Kemble, in the late eighteenth and early nineteenth centuries, at the classical end and Edmund Kean, Kemble's near contemporary, at the romantic end. Samuel Taylor Coleridge wrote that "seeing Kean act was like reading Shakespeare by flashes of lightning." Kean gave his Othello a "tawny" color, and his mature performances were said to combine frightening jealousy and heartrending grief. The fact that the actor himself was charged with adultery caused his audiences to hoot at him when he accused Desdemona of infidelity. Finally, his art and life so converged that in 1833, right after the farewell scene in the third act (Scene 3), Kean collapsed into the arms of his son, who was playing Iago, and was carried from the stage forever.

Among the other famous nineteenth-century Shakespearean actors were Edwin Thomas Booth (brother of Abraham Lincoln's assassin) and Sir Henry Irving, both of whom failed in their Othellos but excelled in their Iagos, who they agreed had to be played coolly, with nothing of the leering villain in him. The greatest Othello of the age was Tommaso Salvini, who spoke in Italian even when performing with English-speaking companies. His performances were praised for their sensuality and violence (he was known to seize Iago by the throat and to fling Desdemona onto the bed). Salvini touched his audiences deeply, even as he terrified them, and people loved him for it.

The first black actor to play Othello professionally was Ira Aldridge. Born in the United States in 1805, Aldridge had to go to England to play in a company with white actors. (In the United States in the nineteenth century, and for a good part of the twentieth, black actors could act only in all-black companies.) Paul Robeson, an African American athlete and concert singer, also went to England to act, performing the part of Othello in 1930. Finally, however, a production of *Othello* with Paul Robeson in the title role, José Ferrer as Iago, and Uta Hagen as Desdemona was mounted in New York in 1943. Although it ran for a record 296 performances, critics disagreed on whether Robeson's accentuation of the racial theme enhanced or diminished the play. In later decades such black actors as Moses Gunn, Paul Winfield, and James Earl Jones gave their own interpretations of Othello in racially mixed American companies.

Apart from Robeson, the best-known twentieth-century Othello is Sir Laurence Olivier, who played the Moor in 1964 in a production with Dame Maggie Smith as Desdemona. Olivier had also played Iago in 1937 in an unusual psychoanalytic interpretation of the play, in which Iago is subconsciously in love with Othello, who was played by Sir Ralph Richardson. That production was not well received.

In the 1964 production, Olivier emphasized Othello's exotic aspects. The actor painted himself very black and walked barefoot on the stage, wearing ankle bracelets and speaking with a musical West Indian accent. In Olivier's interpretation, Othello is a man whose thin layer of civilization is dramatically, but not tragically, stripped from him. It was an astonishing performance that made Iago and Desdemona almost irrelevant. Olivier's *Othello* was filmed in 1965; it stayed close to the stage production and took little advantage of the unique techniques available to filmmaking.

The director and actor Orson Welles, on the other hand, freely added to and adapted the play for his 1955 screen version, inventing a prologue and an epilogue in which we see the funeral processions of Othello and Desdemona from the vantage point of Iago, who is chained in a cage.

In 1981, Jonathan Miller directed Anthony Hopkins in *Othello* for BBC television. Miller, too, saw the play as depicting not a fall from grandeur but "the disintegration of the ordinary, of the representative character. It is the very ordinariness of Othello that makes the story intolerable."

Musical Interpretations

It is not surprising that a play as passionate and as tragic as *Othello* should have inspired two of the greatest nineteenth-century Italian composers of opera: Gioacchino Rossini and Giuseppe Verdi. Rossini's *Otello,* composed in 1816, is rarely performed today, but Verdi's opera, which debuted in La Scala in Milan in 1887, is one of the most famous and highly praised operas in the modern repertoire. Verdi's librettist (writer of the words that accompany the music), Arrigo Boito, also a poet, succeeded in compressing Shakespeare's *Othello* without losing its grandeur and pathos. The work is set entirely on Cyprus and focuses on the conflict among the three major characters, with Verdi's music now conveying the play's great depth of emotion. For example, Verdi gives Desdemona a moving Ave Maria to sing before she dies and uses the contrast of solo and larger vocal units to embody the dramatic tensions between individuals and the community.

Drama Study Guide: The Tragedy of Othello, the Moor of Venice

HRW MATERIAL COPYRIGHTED UNDER NOTICE APPEARING EARLIER IN THIS WORK.

11

Critical Responses to *Othello*

Since its first performance in the early years of the seventeenth century, *Othello* has been one of the most frequently performed of Shakespeare's plays and one that has been highly prized by actors, directors, and audiences. Critics have been less unanimous in their praise and often disagree about the character and the motivation of Othello and Iago and about the overall meaning and morality of the tragedy. Some early critics, like Thomas Rymer in *A Short View of Tragedy* (1692), found the play immoral and incomprehensible. Three hundred years later, Harley Granville-Barker echoed Rymer with his evaluation of *Othello* as "a tragedy without meaning." Some nineteenth-century critics were concerned with the moral ramifications of a play in which goodness and innocence, in the person of Desdemona, are so cruelly and irrevocably destroyed. Others were shocked and repelled by the depiction of the marriage of a white woman and a dark-skinned man, engaging in lengthy debates on just how dark Shakespeare meant Othello to be—whether, in Samuel Taylor Coleridge's words, he was a "veritable Negro" or whether he was merely darker than the European norm.

The prevailing nineteenth-century view of Othello as a noble and suffering hero was challenged in the twentieth century by critics like F. R. Leavis and T. S. Eliot, who saw Othello as a self-dramatizing egotist ruined by his own lack of self-knowledge. Here are excerpts of critical opinion on the characters of Othello, Iago, and Desdemona and on some of the other major issues of the play:

The Character of Othello

The fiery openness of Othello, magnanimous, artless, and credulous, boundless in his confidence, ardent in his affection, inflexible in his resolution, and obdurate in his revenge . . . [is] . . . [proof] of Shakespeare's skill in human nature.

—Samuel Johnson (eighteenth century)

The unsuspecting confidence with which [Othello] listens to his adviser, the agony with which he shrinks from the thought of shame, the tempest of passion with which he commits his crimes, and the haughty fearlessness with which he avows them, give an extraordinary interest to his character.

—Thomas Babington Macaulay, 1827

[Othello] is a union of not merely dissimilar qualities but of dissimilar natures. He is a civilized barbarian.

—William Makepeace Thackeray, 1854

Faults Othello certainly has, but it is often difficult not to feel that his tragedy springs most deeply from his very magnanimity, with which he is so embarrassingly endowed that he trusts Iago.

—Willard Farnham, 1936

Othello's freedom from suspicion which is based on his own transparent sincerity leads to an absurd credulity and it reveals an ignorance of human nature. His pride in his own achievements and his sense of honor are linked with the common delusion that a man's honor can be smirched by his wife's misbehavior and redeemed only by her death. Above all, he is too confident of his own rationality.

—Kenneth Muir, 1968

Othello is a patient rather than an agent, worked on by forces outside himself, as total a victim of deception as any character in the Shakespearean canon.

—Norman Sanders, 1984

The Character of Iago

Iago is . . . of diseased intellectual activity, with an almost perfect indifference to moral good or evil, or rather with a decided preference of the latter. . . . He runs all risks for a trifling and doubtful advantage and is himself the dupe and victim of his ruling passion—an insatiable craving after action of the most difficult and dangerous kind.

—William Hazlitt, 1817

The last speech [Iago's soliloquy at the end of Act I], the motive-hunting of motiveless malignity—how awful! . . . A being next to devil, only not quite devil.

—Samuel Taylor Coleridge (nineteenth century)

To his bad eminence above all other figures of evil in the Elizabethan drama [Iago] is elevated not only by the shock of his turpitude, the pathos of his victims, and the poetry of his role, but also, and in no small measure, by his mystery.

—Bernard Spivack, 1958

The secret of Iago is not a motiveless malignity—though, being evil, he has a natural hatred of good—but a pathological jealousy of his wife, a suspicion of every man with whom she is acquainted, and a jealous love of Desdemona.

—Kenneth Muir, 1968

*Drama Study Guide: **The Tragedy of Othello, the Moor of Venice***

The Character of Desdemona

Desdemona, with all her timid flexibility and soft acquiescence, is not weak; for the negative alone is weak, and the mere presence of goodness and affection implies in itself a species of power—power without consciousness, power without effort, power with repose—that soul of grace!

—Anna Brownell Jameson, 1833

[Desdemona] is a life force that strives for order, community, growth, and light.

—Alvin Kernan, 1963

Assumption of responsibility for her own fate turns into something perilously close to masochism; . . . a love that transcends all ordinary limits results in the passive acceptance of death at its loss.

—Norman Sanders, 1984

Othello's Color

[Desdemona] sees Othello's color in his mind. But upon the stage, when the imagination is no longer the ruling faculty, but we are left to our poor, unassisted senses, I appeal to everyone that has seen *Othello* played, whether he did not . . . find something extremely revolting in the courtship and wedded caresses of Othello and Desdemona.

—Charles Lamb, 1810

It would be something monstrous to conceive this beautiful Venetian girl falling in love with a veritable Negro. It would argue a disproportionateness, a want of balance, in Desdemona, which Shakespeare does not appear to have in the least contemplated.

—Samuel Taylor Coleridge (nineteenth century)

The problem [of *Othello*] is the problem of my own people. It is a tragedy of racial conflict, a tragedy of honor, rather than of jealousy.

—Paul Robeson (twentieth century)

It is of the very essence of the play that Desdemona in marrying Othello—a man to whom her "natural" reaction should (her father holds) have been fear, not delight—has done something peculiarly startling.

—M. R. Ridley, 1958

Given Coleridge's certainty that Othello could not possibly have been black, it is well to reiterate that the Elizabethans thought of Moors as black.

—Sylvan Barnet, 1963

It is significant that only Iago and Brabantio seem to have any color prejudice against Othello.

—Kenneth Muir, 1968

The Ending of the Play

What Othello seems to be doing in making this [last] speech is *cheering himself up*. He is endeavoring to escape reality, he has ceased to think about Desdemona, and is thinking about himself . . . dramatizing himself against his environment. He takes in the spectator, but the human motive is to take in himself.

—T. S. Eliot, 1932

The end is most moving. Othello is purged of all personal animosity. He sees Desdemona's death as a duty laid on him, and he does not consult his own heart when duty is concerned. . . . Then, too late, he learns the truth, and his universe falls about him.

—G. B. Harrison, 1948

The Othello who sends his last message to the senate and dies upon a kiss is again the Othello who stood before the senate in Venice and greeted Desdemona in Cyprus.

—M. R. Ridley, 1958

Drama Study Guide: The Tragedy of Othello, the Moor of Venice

HRW MATERIAL COPYRIGHTED UNDER NOTICE APPEARING EARLIER IN THIS WORK.

13

Elements of the Play

Key Literary Elements of the Play

Protagonists: Othello, Desdemona, Cassio

Antagonist: Iago

Conflicts: person versus person; person versus society; person versus self

Significant Techniques: blank verse, figurative language, imagery, punning, allusion, soliloquy, dramatic and situational irony, suspense, foreshadowing

Setting: Venice and Cyprus (an island in the Mediterranean Sea, off the southern coast of what is now Turkey)

The Themes of *Othello*

Appearance Versus Reality

Of Othello, Iago says, "The Moor is of a free and open nature / That thinks men honest that but seem to be so" (Act I, Scene 3, lines 391–392), and where Iago is concerned, all the other characters share the same inability to distinguish his presentation of himself from his true nature. Only the audience, with the advantage of hearing Iago speak his mind in soliloquies, can discern his double-dealing.

Othello, of course, makes a far less understandable mistake in judging Desdemona guilty of infidelity simply because things on the surface do not appear to be as they should be—Cassio slips away from Desdemona when Othello approaches; Bianca is in possession of Desdemona's handkerchief. Shakespeare seems to be asking whether we can ever be sure of our knowledge of another (all who admired Othello as a noble and disciplined man are amazed at his transformation into a jealous killer) and, according to the critic Kenneth Muir, whether we are not all forced on some level to present ourselves to others in social roles as though we were actors performing onstage.

Jealousy and Betrayal

The play abounds with instances of jealousy of all kinds—professional, sexual, and personal. Iago is angered first by Cassio's promotion to a job he believes he deserves. Later he reveals a more generalized envy of Cassio, seeming to recognize in him what is lacking in himself: "He hath a daily beauty in his life / That makes me ugly" (Act V, Scene 1, lines 19–20). Like Iago and Othello, Bianca is also quick to imagine that her beloved (Cassio) is playing her false. Othello's homicidal jealousy, however, is the central mystery of the play. Is Shakespeare telling us that jealousy is a force so powerful that it can undermine the noblest of natures, or is Othello a victim of some weakness—pride or personal insecurity or an inability, as some critics have suggested, to live with doubt or uncertainty? Samuel Johnson thought that Othello is not particularly jealous at all but instead so skillfully played upon by Iago that he is eventually inflamed. Whatever weaknesses in Othello Iago manipulates, it is Iago, not Desdemona, who betrays Othello's trust and succeeds in putting Othello "into a jealousy so strong / That judgment cannot cure" (Act II, Scene 1, lines 297–298).

Love

This is a play about love, and according to the critic Rosalie L. Colie, "The lovers are not star-crossed but crossed by their own personalities, by their own natures." All agree that Desdemona's love for Othello is strong and true, although some critics have faulted her naiveté and her lack of self-protective instincts in continuing to plead for Cassio and choosing to lie about the handkerchief to a clearly jealous husband. In Desdemona's dialogue with Emilia on the night of her murder, her innocence and idealism about marital love seem otherworldly in contrast to her maidservant's down-to-earth realism. Emilia's love for Iago is conditional; she loves him until she has convincing evidence that he has harmed someone she loves, Desdemona. Cassio's love for Bianca is also pragmatic, whereas Othello's love for Desdemona is passionate and all-encompassing.

Kenneth Muir has argued that Othello is slow to succumb to jealousy and that even in the grip of suspicious rage he never stops loving Desdemona. Othello's devastation on realizing his terrible delusion was so moving for one of Shakespeare's contemporaries, Ben Jonson, that he found the last scene "unendurable." The love Shakespeare dramatizes in *Othello* is surely powerful, but it is also destructive of both individual and communal peace.

Cast of Characters in the Play

Main Characters

OTHELLO, a soldier of fortune from North Africa, is employed as a general by the city-state of Venice. Although he is respected by the Venetian nobility for his military skill and personal integrity, as a man of color and a foreigner he will always be an outsider, no matter what his personal virtues and his value to the state. One Venetian, however, accepts him without reserve—his wife, Desdemona—and he responds with a full-hearted love of his own, making her the center of his emotional universe.

In the course of the play, Othello moves from a confident, self-controlled leader and loving husband to a suspicious, vengeful destroyer of what he loves most. But his character development doesn't end here; he goes on to acknowledge his monstrous error and to experience a terrible remorse. The audience and some of the other characters recall his greatness and are moved to pity his steep fall from grace. In fact, of all Shakespeare's tragic heroes, Othello is the easiest to identify with because, according to the critic M. R. Ridley, he is undone by a powerful emotion, jealousy, that plagues us all.

DESDEMONA, daughter of a Venetian nobleman, is a beautiful and accomplished young woman, protected by her father. She is captivated by the older, less polished Othello, whose life has been different from her own—full of adventures, hardships, and opportunities for courageous action. Despite her inexperience, Desdemona shows courage by marrying Othello and committing herself to him totally despite her father's disapproval. In the play, Desdemona stands for love, trust, and purity—all that makes life meaningful and worth living—while her foil, Iago, stands for all that is destructive of life.

Unlike Othello, Desdemona does not change in the course of the play. Her love for, and devotion to, her husband is unwavering; she doesn't even accuse him of her murder.

For this reason she is sometimes played as naive or one-dimensional, but as Ridley has pointed out, she defied convention in marrying Othello, and "she can stand up to Othello, for the sake of what she thinks to be right, even when he is in a dangerous mood." Othello himself calls her "my fair warrior" (Act II, Scene 1, line 178).

IAGO, Othello's ancient, or ensign, wishes to become Othello's second in command but is passed over in favor of the aristocratic Cassio. Determined to get revenge, Iago pretends to be the loyal subordinate while plotting to destroy all that Othello values. On the allegorical, or symbolic, level, Iago stands for evil or for man's lower nature, driven by greed, lust, envy, and hatred.

The critical debate over Iago's character centers on whether Shakespeare has provided credible psychological motivation to explain the sheer destructiveness of Iago's plotting. To critics like Samuel Taylor Coleridge, the only motive for Iago's scheming is the pleasure of doing evil. For most contemporary critics, however, Iago is surely a villain, but a human one, psychologically complex and convincing, not an inhuman connoisseur of evil for its own sake.

BRABANTIO, the father of Desdemona, is a Venetian nobleman and senator. He is a proud, generous, and conventional patriarch who has lovingly raised his daughter with every advantage but also with the expectation that she will do what she is told. He is horrified when his well-brought-up daughter defies him and her social class by marrying a dark-skinned foreigner.

Some directors and critics have seen Brabantio as a bit of a fool, along the lines of Polonius in *Hamlet,* but most agree that Shakespeare and his audience would have found nothing unreasonable in this father's vexation at his daughter's surprising choice of a husband.

Drama Study Guide: The Tragedy of Othello, the Moor of Venice

HRW MATERIAL COPYRIGHTED UNDER NOTICE APPEARING EARLIER IN THIS WORK.

15

CASSIO, the gentleman soldier, is a man of ability, loyalty, and grace. He is of high social rank, a Florentine with all the polish and social advantages that go with high birth. Like Othello he is not a native Venetian but is embraced on his merits by the Venetian nobility. His admiration for Desdemona is genuine and undesigning, as is his respect and affection for Othello. But like Othello, too, he has a lower nature—under the influence of alcohol, he becomes irrational and violent. He cannot see through Iago and is unduly influenced by him. Of the major characters he alone has the opportunity at the end of the play to rebuild his life and his reputation.

EMILIA, maidservant to Desdemona and wife of Iago, is a woman of common sense and ordinary decency who is loyal to her mistress and to her husband until she has good reason to be otherwise. Unlike Desdemona she is no paragon of virtue. She willingly lies and steals at her husband's request but, according to Ridley, is kindled by Desdemona's murder to "a bright flame of self-forgetful courage," dismissing both Othello and her husband as "irrelevant trivialities."

RODERIGO, a Venetian gentleman in love with Desdemona, is distinguished only by his complete willingness to be led on by Iago's promises of getting Desdemona away from Othello. He ends up handing over the jewels he has bought for her and, finally, his life without gaining anything for himself. His credulity is a perverse reflection of Othello's. Roderigo is without a doubt the "gull," "dolt," and "fool" that Emilia labels Othello (Act V, Scene 2, lines 163 and 233).

Supporting Characters

BIANCA, mistress to Cassio.

MONTANO, Othello's predecessor as governor of Cyprus.

GRATIANO, a noble Venetian and brother to Brabantio.

LODOVICO, a noble Venetian and kinsman to Brabantio.

SENATORS of Venice.

CLOWN, servant to Othello.

SAILOR, MESSENGER, HERALD, OFFICERS, GENTLEMEN, MUSICIANS, and ATTENDANTS.

The Setting

The play has two major settings: the sixteenth-century city-state of Venice and the island of Cyprus, at the time of the play a possession of the Venetian maritime empire. The action moves from Venice to Cyprus and then psychologically, though not literally, back to Venice. According to the critic Alvin Kernan, the geography of the play mirrors the psychological journey of the characters.

At the beginning the characters are in the civilized and secure confines of Venice, ruled by a Senate of rational men committed to civil order. Othello, although he comes from an unknown foreign place, demonstrates the confident self-discipline of one who has met and faced down the forces of barbarism, and so the Venetians rely on him to protect them from the infidel Turks, who are bearing down on their empire by sea.

In the second act, Othello departs from the safety of Venice, braves the natural forces of the sea, and lands in Cyprus, an outpost of Venice where the refinements of city life are a pale imitation of those in the capital. Here rationality, discipline, and order break down, and barbarism in the form of jealousy, murder, and revenge takes hold. All the gentlemen—Othello, Cassio, Roderigo—descend to violence in Cyprus. Finally, with the arrival of Lodovico and Gratiano from the capital, the order of Venice is reimposed on the chaos of Cyprus. Civilization reasserts itself as Iago is exposed and vilified, a repentant Othello acts as his own judge and executioner, and Cassio assumes control of the island on the orders of the Senate.

A Tragic Plot

Of Shakespeare's four greatest tragedies (*Hamlet, King Lear, Othello,* and *Macbeth*), *Othello* is often considered the greatest play in the sense of effective theater but not the greatest work. *Othello*'s success as drama has been explained by its near total adherence to the three unities recommended by Aristotle in his *Poetics:* time, place, and action. Events move quickly in *Othello;* by one reckoning the momentous action in Cyprus takes place in a mere thirty-six hours. The main setting shifts only once (from Venice to Cyprus). And there are no subplots and practically no comic—or any other—relief from the relentless movement toward disaster.

In addition to the intensity created by this concentration of action and emotion, the domestic, or close-to-home, nature of the conflict is bound to move audiences all too familiar with the pains of love and jealousy.

The structure of the action in *Othello,* however, is essentially the same as that of the other great Shakespearean tragedies. As presented in critic A. C. Bradley's classic 1904 analysis of Shakespearean tragedy, all four plays have a falling action that begins with the exposition of the hero's situation and character and moves through conflict, crisis, and catastrophe to a final denouement, or relaxation of dramatic tension. Although there is a feeling of inevitability in the movement toward the death of the hero, as in Greek tragedy, in Shakespeare there is also a sense of human responsibility, of a hero who, in Bradley's view, is both noble and flawed and has had a hand in his own fate. Yet Bradley saw in *Othello* a weakness he did not see in the other three tragedies; that is, *Othello* "has not . . . the power of dilating the imagination by vague suggestions of huge universal powers working in the world of individual fate and passion."

Contemporary critics have looked at the structure of Shakespeare's tragedies in different ways. For example, Maynard Mack, in his essay "The Jacobean Shakespeare," sees a structure in which the hero, in his attempt to transcend the limits of ordinary life or love, overreaches and loses his better self and ultimately his life. But that is not the end of the tragic trajectory, in Mack's view: Before his death the hero is allowed to recover something of his former nobility. Of Othello he writes, "It will be given to the hero to recapture the faith he lost, to learn that the pearl was really richer than all his tribe."

The Language

In addition to exploring the structure of the dramatic action, contemporary critics have called attention to the verbal structures, or patterns of imagery, that unify the play and articulate its themes. For not only is *Othello* great drama, but it is great poetry as well. In fact, Shakespeare gives each of the major characters a distinct idiom, which is a kind of key to his or her nature.

What the critic G. Wilson Knight called the "Othello music" is stately, romantic, picturesque, and capable of deep emotion. In contrast, Iago's characteristic speech (expressed more often in prose than poetry) is clipped, controlled, intellectual, and fashioned for a purpose. Where Othello inflates, Iago deflates. The contrast in their characters is initially reflected in the dichotomous imagery associated with them. The newly married Othello inhabits a world of color, love, and heavenly grace, whereas Iago's world is dark, infernal, and inhabited by men who act like beasts. As Iago succeeds in poisoning Othello's mind, Othello increasingly adopts Iago's characteristic imagery and mixes it with his own in speeches like this one, addressed to Desdemona, which displays his tormented inner conflict:

> The fountain from the which my current runs
> Or else dries up—to be discarded thence,
> Or keep it as a cistern for foul toads
> To knot and gender in—turn thy complexion
>   there,
> Patience, thou young and rose-lipped cherubin!
>   —Act IV, Scene 2, lines 58–62

Patterns of contrasting images (light and dark, white and black, day and night, heaven and hell) also suffuse the play and transcend association with any one character. They reflect and illuminate the thematic tensions between being and seeming, loving and hating, fidelity and betrayal. Other repeated motifs include war and the military, infection and disease, magic and witchcraft, and trials and torture. Together they create a system of meaning that supports and fulfills the structure of the action.

Teaching the Play

Objectives

1. To gain exposure to Shakespeare's life and work and to Elizabethan stage conventions
2. To improve reading proficiency and expand vocabulary
3. To recognize how the play relates to contemporary life
4. To identify details of plot, setting, and characterization
5. To respond to the play, orally and in writing
6. To identify and define dramatic and poetic techniques
7. To write an interior monologue, an essay about women in the play, a response to a review of the play, an analysis of a character in the play, a response to a review of a film or stage performance, a description of the staging of the play, and a prequel to the play
8. To practice critical thinking and critical writing skills

Introducing the Play

Shakespearean Drama

Students who have enjoyed other tragedies by Shakespeare—*Romeo and Juliet, Julius Caesar, Macbeth*—will find some surprises in *Othello.*

There are fewer allusions to supernatural powers—no ghosts, as in *Macbeth* and *Hamlet;* no witches or soothsayers to foretell the future, as in *Macbeth* and *Julius Caesar;* and no chorus to announce the fate of the star-crossed lovers. Nor does the action take place within a known historical period, as is the case in the Roman tragedies. There are no offstage battles to decide a hero's fate. In this play the hero seems to have his fate in his own hands. The catastrophe in *Othello* arises from the decisions the characters make and from their natures.

To introduce your students to this play, point out that Shakespeare took many of his plots from older literature and from history, and he wrote mainly to move and entertain his contemporaries. What playgoers crowding the Globe Theater responded to was Shakespeare's subtle and fascinating characters; his fast-moving, suspenseful plots; his sharp humor; his power to evoke a world with words—all the things that audiences respond to today. Reassure your students that they will find these elements in *Othello.*

Reassure them, too, that all modern readers need help understanding Shakespeare's language and his literary, topical, and historical allusions. And let your students know that they will get the help they need, from the text and from you.

The Five-Part Dramatic Structure

In your introduction to the play, also discuss the five-part dramatic structure, corresponding generally (although not absolutely) to the play's five acts. You may want to duplicate for your students the following diagram and definitions.

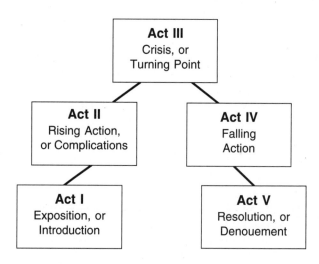

The **exposition,** or **introduction,** establishes tone, setting, some of the main characters, previous events necessary for understanding the play's action, and the main **conflict,** or problem.

*Drama Study Guide: **The Tragedy of Othello, the Moor of Venice***

The **rising action** is a series of **complications** besetting the protagonist that arise when the protagonist takes action to resolve his or her main conflict.

The **crisis,** or **turning point,** is the moment of choice for the protagonist, the moment when the forces of conflict come together and the situation will either improve or inexorably deteriorate. The crisis usually occurs in Act III.

The **falling action** presents the incidents resulting from the protagonist's decision at the turning point. In tragedy these incidents necessarily emphasize the play's destructive forces but often include an episode of possible salvation, as well as comic scenes. These are the playwright's means of maintaining suspense and relieving the tension as the catastrophe approaches.

The **resolution,** or **denouement,** is the conclusion of the play, the unraveling of the plot, which in tragedy includes the **catastrophe** of the hero's and others' deaths. The **climax,** or emotional peak, usually occurs right before the denouement.

The Appeal of the Play

Othello is a powerful, exciting, and deeply felt tragedy. It holds the attention of its audience whenever actors have succeeded in responding to its challenges, and students are bound to get caught up in it. There is evidence that it was performed more often in Shakespeare's day than any of his other tragedies were. One reason for the play's early appeal was Shakespeare's choice of Venice as the initial setting. To Shakespeare's contemporaries, Venice was an exotic, corrupt—as well as beautiful and cultured—place. The effect of this setting is further heightened by the hero, Othello, a Moor who commands respect and arouses wonder but also suggests destruction and suffering.

But neither the appeal of the setting nor the mystery of the hero is sufficient to account for the enduring popularity of the play. It is the excitement of the action that holds audiences and readers today. The pace of the play picks up as the action progresses and speeds to its disastrous conclusion. The dramatic focus narrows—from the streets and the senate of Venice to the citadel at Cyprus and finally to Desdemona's bedchamber—and Shakespeare's language becomes more intense, with the use of words like *fool, devil, soul, body, good,* and *heart* repeated over and over until they resound on the stage.

Reading and Performing the Play

Some teachers like to plunge their students immediately into a brief "performance" of the play. If you want to try this, assign parts for an informal performance of the opening scene of Act I—the mysterious meeting of two figures in the night. True darkness is not necessary; just instruct students to use gestures and voices that suggest nighttime. Remember that these two figures are meeting secretly and that this is the quiet and mysterious beginning to a sinister drama.

Don't have a rehearsal; just get two students up in front of the class, books in hand, and have them read their parts. You can have several groups take turns performing the scene. You'll undoubtedly be surprised at how quickly the students catch on to the action and how quickly, with a few of these impromptu performances, some of the hurdles to the language are cleared.

When you assign the reading of Act I, go over the format of the text carefully. Show students that unfamiliar words, phrases, and allusions are marked with a symbol and explained in a footnote that is keyed to the appropriate line number. Next, read a few of the Guided Reading questions, which begin on page 34 of this guide. Explain that these questions aid understanding by pointing to details of the plot and eliciting interpretations of character, language, and staging.

Use the first class period after students have read the act to allow them to *hear* Shakespeare's language. Read the opening scene yourself, play a recording, or show a film. This will provide a model of correct phrasing and will show how much an actor's interpretation adds to the play's meaning.

A resource that is full of good ideas about teaching the play by means of performance is the Folger Library's *Shakespeare Set Free,* edited by Peggy O'Brien (Washington Square Press, published by Pocket Books).

Understanding the Literary Elements

Remind students of the genre they are studying: Drama is a literary *and* a performing art. *Othello,* though written to be acted, is splendid reading. As you read, play recordings, and show films, students should see how gestures, timing, staging, sound effects, and actors' interpretations can affect meaning. Although the words do not change from performance to performance, the audience's perceptions and reactions do. The questions and exercises in this Study Guide will help students appreciate Shakespeare's mastery of dramatic structure and literary techniques. By reading and studying this play, students should come to see how Shakespeare keeps the audience's interest—how he alternates scenes of psychological subtlety with emotional peaks, how complex his characters are (Iago, though driven by passion and hatred, is also clever and cold), how exquisitely he uses language (his verse is filled with irony, imagery, and vivid figures of speech).

Establishing a Procedure

Before you begin to teach *Othello,* examine the teaching resources in this Study Guide; they provide a wealth of ideas for classroom work, homework assignments, projects, reports, and tests. If possible, obtain a film of *Othello,* as well as books and audiovisual materials about Shakespeare, his times, and the Globe Theater. Then, determine which projects and writing exercises you will assign at the beginning of the unit, decide how you will present each act, and prepare a daily reading and assignment schedule. If possible, allow four weeks for the study of the play.

Use the first two or three days to prepare students for the reading. Discuss the Introduction to the HRW Classics edition of *Othello* (pages 1–14), and enhance the historical information with filmstrips, films, or illustrated books. Do not let your students be intimidated by the poetry of the play; introduce terms and read passages aloud, but postpone scrutiny of the dramatic technique until they are interested in the play and more comfortable with its language. In the same way, briefly introduce the five-part structure of Shakespearean drama. In doing this, you will be providing your students with a vocabulary for discussing form, which they will do with much more understanding as they follow the plot.

Finally, distribute your schedule for the play, and explain long-range projects and writing exercises. For example, if you want the class to undertake small-group activities, you should assign students to groups at this point so that members of groups can begin working together.

Here is a suggested procedure for presenting each act of the play. Before students begin reading, establish the time and the place of each scene (if you wish, summarize the plot or distribute a plot summary); assign vocabulary words, discussion questions, and any writing exercises; designate passages for oral reading; alert students to any scenes for which you will play a recording; and remind students of quizzes and scheduled reports.

Schedule at least two days of class time for each act, with the exception of Act III, which will require three days. Vary activities from act to act as much as possible. The suggested combination of oral readings, discussion, viewings of scenes, and project reports should keep students stimulated throughout the course of the play.

After students finish reading the play, show a filmed production straight through; students will by then know the play very well, and the viewing will synthesize their experience of its elements.

Providing for Different Levels of Ability

Work individually with students who have particular difficulty with Shakespeare's language, and emphasize paraphrasing in both written and oral work. To prepare students with limited English, have them make full use of plot summaries, vocabulary definitions, and audiovisual aids in conjunction with small-group projects and writing exercises.

Additional options for teaching the play are described, act by act, beginning on page 21 of this Study Guide.

Options for Teaching the Play

Use these ideas to modify your instruction to suit the needs of individual students.

Act I

Strategies for Inclusion

ENGLISH LANGUAGE DEVELOPMENT Use frequent check tests to be sure students are comprehending the text. Ask students to stop at intervals and answer these or similar questions:

1. Who is speaking?
2. What is the character talking about?
3. To whom is the character speaking?
4. Who else is onstage?

LESS PROFICIENT READERS When you assign the reading of Act I, go over the format of the text carefully. Show students that unfamiliar words, phrases, and allusions are marked with a symbol and explained in a footnote by line number. Read aloud a few of the Guided Reading questions, which begin on page 34 of this guide, and explain that these questions aid understanding by pointing to plot details and eliciting interpretations of character, language, theme, and staging.

VISUAL/LINGUISTIC To help students use prior knowledge to interpret the play, ask them to share their first thoughts on several main-idea words from Act I. List on the chalkboard, one at a time, such key words as *love, hate, trust, war, reality,* and *lies.* From students' suggestions, make a cluster diagram like the following one.

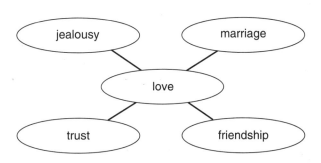

SPATIAL To help students track the sequence of events in the first scenes, ask them to write the scene numbers at the tops of sheets of paper, one scene to a page (they may also want to use a different-colored sheet of paper for each scene). When they finish reading a scene, discuss the events as a class. Then, have each student write on his or her appropriately labeled sheet of paper a short summary of the action that has taken place. Students may also want to list on their scene pages

the characters in the scene and add an illustration or a graphic organizer to help them keep the action of the story clear.

Integrating the Language Arts

STRATEGIC READING Before students begin reading, review the organization of a play (stage directions, the list of characters, the dialogue). Also review the format for recording a reference to a particular line so that students will be able to refer to lines and scenes properly in their writing and take notes more efficiently.

In reviewing how lines are counted, point out the difference between prose speeches (for example, Act I, Scene 3, lines 219–226) and verse. Show the class that in prose every line is assigned a number whereas in verse, turnover lines count for only one line even though they take up a second line on the page. Use Act I, Scene 1, lines 50–55, as an example. Then, ask students to look for examples of split lines, and ask volunteers to explain how they are counted. Challenge students to find in Act I a single line that is spoken by three characters (for example, Scene 3, lines 238 and 274).

Note that act numbers are represented by capital Roman numerals and line numbers are generally written in Arabic numerals. Scene numbers are represented by either Arabic numerals or lowercase Roman numerals. The act number always appears first, the scene number second, and the line number(s) third.

So that the class can practice citing passages from *Othello,* read aloud the following famous lines. Ask students to write down the lines, locate them, and then write the correct act, scene, and line numbers next to each one.

> But I will wear my heart upon my sleeve
> For daws to peck at. I am not what I am.
>> (Act I, Scene 1, lines 62–63)

> To mourn a mischief that is past and gone
> Is the next way to draw new mischief on.
>> (Act I, Scene 3, lines 202–203)

> The robbed that smiles steals something from the thief.
>> (Act I, Scene 3, line 206)

> My life upon her faith! Honest Iago . . .
>> (Act I, Scene 3, line 290)

*Drama Study Guide: **The Tragedy of Othello, the Moor of Venice***

SPEAKING AND LISTENING Discuss with students the differences between reading a story aloud and reading a play aloud, focusing on characterization through speech. Review elements of speech such as pitch, tone, articulation, accent, and pace. Assign specific passages to students, and have them practice on their own before reading them aloud in class. Remind students that you expect them to use the elements of speech mentioned above to dramatize their prepared readings.

Cooperative Learning

CHARACTER SOCIOGRAMS To help students distinguish among the characters and understand their relationships to one another, have the class work in groups to create character sociograms. Instruct students to write in separate boxes the name of each main character introduced in the opening act—Othello, Iago, Desdemona, Cassio, and Brabantio. Then, have them write, on arrows drawn between the boxes, words that describe the relationships between the two characters. Finally, ask students to provide one quote from the play to support each description.

THEMATIC AWARENESS Divide the class into three groups, and let each group choose one of the following themes.

1. People are not always what they seem to be.

2. Jealousy can cause harm.

3. Good people sometimes behave badly.

Have each group follow its theme through the play, identifying pertinent speeches. Periodically, ask each group to report its findings to the class.

Classroom Management

BASE GROUPS To help students master Shakespeare's language, understand the plot line, and analyze the themes, assign them to base groups—cooperative learning groups that will remain intact throughout the teaching of this play. Ideally you should form the groups, assigning to each group two to four students of mixed levels or ability. As the class does vocabulary exercises, paraphrases passages, or answers discussion questions, individual students may need help, and they will benefit from consultation with the other members of their base group.

BLOCK SCHEDULING When assigning research projects, encourage students to take advantage of the library's many resources. Give the class a tour of the local library. Point out the different areas where sound and video recordings, reference books, and literary works are shelved. If possible, use an extended class period to allow students to begin conducting research.

Crossing the Curriculum

MUSIC Have students working in groups locate recorded music that can be used to create an appropriate mood for each act of the play. Remind the class to review the major events in each act in order to identify the atmosphere. Have students share their selections with the class and explain why they chose them.

Consider playing some of these musical selections as students enter or leave the classroom or as they work on group activities.

ARCHITECTURE Students might be interested in finding out more about Elizabethan theaters. Have the class work in small groups to research the Globe. Topics might be narrowed to outside appearance, seating arrangements, mechanical devices such as trapdoors, and sections of the stage. In presentations to the class, groups should make use of visual representations. Encourage interested students to construct a model theater from a kit.

Assessment Tools

CHECK TEST: QUESTIONS AND ANSWERS

1. In the opening scene, why do Iago and Roderigo rush to Brabantio's house? [They want to tell Brabantio that his daughter, Desdemona, has eloped with Othello.]

2. Why does Roderigo enjoy giving Brabantio the news of the elopement? [As a suitor of Desdemona's, Roderigo was rejected by Brabantio. Now he is taking revenge, telling the older man something he knows will hurt him.]

3. Of what city is Othello the leading military figure? [He is the leading military figure of Venice.]

4. What army appears to be planning an invasion of Cyprus? [The Turkish army appears to be planning an invasion.]

5. What political office does Brabantio hold? [He is a senator.]

6. In whose care is Desdemona left at the end of Act I? [She is left in Iago's care.]

INFORMAL ASSESSMENT To determine whether students are using the language of the play to respond to questions and to participate in class discussions, rate students on a scale of one to five (five points being the best), using the following three criteria:

1 Students use important words from the play (for example, theme words).

2 Students quote appropriate lines from the play.

3 Students cite passages correctly.

Drama Study Guide: The Tragedy of Othello, the Moor of Venice

Act II

Strategies for Inclusion

SPATIAL To help track the activity that takes place in Act II, have students make columns on a sheet of paper and then add the following headings: "On the Shore in Cyprus," "A Street in Cyprus," and "The Citadel in Cyprus." Then instruct them to take notes as they read, listing each event that occurs in each location.

LESS PROFICIENT READERS To focus students' attention on significant ideas and facts, provide a limited number of preview questions to be answered as the class reads Act II. Questions should be limited to the pertinent facts and concepts and presented in sequential order. It may be helpful to have students copy down each question on a separate card and clip it to the page on which the answer can be found.

Integrating the Language Arts

GRAMMAR Ask partners to list adjectives that describe Iago and to prepare an explanation of each adjective they choose. Then, ask volunteers to present one adjective and the rationale for its selection. Write these adjectives on the chalkboard, and instruct students to use at least five of them in a character sketch of Iago.

STRATEGIC READING Assign pairs of students scenes from Act II to read carefully. Then, have one student in each pair ask his or her partner questions about the reading, and have the partner answer as many of these questions as possible. Then, instruct the partners to reverse roles. To conclude, ask one student in each pair to summarize the scene.

MECHANICS Ask the class to study the text to find devices that Shakespeare used to add or subtract syllables from words to make ten-syllable lines. Invite students to rewrite a story in lines of ten syllables, using some of Shakespeare's devices to make the language fit the format. [Devices include contractions, grave accents, and changes in word forms.]

LANGUAGE AND VOCABULARY As a class, analyze a short passage, and identify words that are not used today or whose meanings have changed. List each word on the chalkboard, and ask students to suggest a more modern word for each. Re-read the passage aloud, substituting the modern words for the archaic ones. Then, ask students what they think of the sound of the updated passage.

Cooperative Learning

CREATE SUMMARIES OF SCENES Choose as many key scenes from Act II as there are cooperative learning groups in your class, and assign one to each group. Have groups write summaries of their scenes to share with the class. Then, call on volunteers to assemble these synopses into a handy reference book.

ANALYZE DIFFICULT LINES Ask students to note lines in Act II they find difficult to comprehend. Later, encourage students to work together to analyze these difficult lines.

QUESTION SLIPS Give students an opportunity to submit anonymous questions about things they do not understand about the play. These can help you clear up misconceptions.

Assessment Tools

CHECK TEST: QUESTIONS AND ANSWERS

1. Why have Cassio, Iago, Desdemona, and Othello left Venice? [They are headed for Cyprus—to head off the Turkish army.]
2. In Scene 1, whose ship appears to be lost in a storm? [Othello's ship seems to be lost.]
3. What falsehood does Iago convince Roderigo of in Scene 1? [He convinces Roderigo that Desdemona is in love with Cassio.]
4. What does a messenger announce in Scene 2? [The messenger, or herald, announces a festival to celebrate the destruction of the Turkish fleet.]
5. How does Iago create the illusion that Cassio is unfit for duty? [He gets Cassio drunk, incites a brawl, makes Cassio look like the instigator.]
6. What is the result of the brawl? [Othello strips Cassio of his rank.]

OBSERVATION ASSESSMENT As students discuss **themes** revealed in Acts I and II, note whether they are making specific references to echoes and repetitions in the text. The following scale may help you make your evaluations.

1 Student discusses the text generally or inaccurately.
2 Student speaks generally, with some mention of lines or scenes.
3 Student refers to lines or scenes but without making specific references.
4 Student occasionally supports discussion with specific references.
5 Student frequently supports discussion with specific references.

*Drama Study Guide: **The Tragedy of Othello, the Moor of Venice***

Act III

Strategies for Inclusion

LESS PROFICIENT READERS Before students begin reading this act, review the style used in recording references to particular lines. Familiarity with the style will enable students to take notes more quickly and easily. Explain how lines are counted. Point out that in a split line the number appears only once, even though the line includes the speech of two or more characters. Note that act numbers are represented by capital Roman numerals, line numbers by Arabic numerals, scene numbers by either Arabic or lowercase Roman numerals. Remind students that the act number always appears first, the scene number second, and the line numbers third.

ENGLISH LANGUAGE DEVELOPMENT To help students follow the **plot,** have them keep a time line of the events that take place. Pause periodically to review what has happened in the play.

STRATEGIC READING To encourage the class to examine events and speculate about their long-range consequences, have students stop at the end of Scene 1 and write a prediction journal entry. Tell students to draw a line down the middle of a sheet of paper. Have them write the heading *What Happened* on the left side, and the heading *What Might Happen As a Result of This Event* on the right side. Discuss students' predictions with the class. Then, after students read Scene 2, ask them to return to their journals and compare their predictions with what actually happens.

SPEAKING AND LISTENING To develop students' metacognitive abilities, try an oral composition activity. Have each student choose a partner; then give each student in a pair a different interpretive essay question about the play (for example, How could a noble man like Othello become consumed with jealousy? Why do so many of the characters trust Iago?). Tell students to take turns speaking (composing aloud an answer to a question) and listening (silently interpreting and recording the speaker's thoughts). Then, tell the students in each pair to exchange and discuss their notes.

MECHANICS Explain to students that a dash is used to indicate a pause—an abrupt break in thought or speech, an unfinished statement or question, or an interruption by another character. Point out that pauses are used for dramatic effect. To demonstrate, ask students to read lines containing dashes as if the dashes were not there and then to read the same lines as written, with the dashes.

Cooperative Learning

CHARACTER SOCIOGRAMS Have students work in groups of three or four to create character sociograms, graphics containing symbols and words that show the relationships between characters. Tell students to include all the characters they have read about in the play, and challenge them to be creative in choosing symbols to show how each character relates to the others.

Assessment Tools

CHECK TEST: QUESTIONS AND ANSWERS

1. Who insults the musicians Cassio has hired to greet Othello? [A clown employed by Othello insults the musicians.]
2. To whom does Othello give letters to be sent to senators in Venice? [He gives the letters to Iago.]
3. Who promises Cassio that she will persuade Othello to reconcile with him? [Desdemona assures Cassio that she will persuade her husband to forgive him.]
4. What suspicion does Iago plant in Othello's mind in Act III, Scene 3? [Iago plants the suspicion in Othello's mind that Cassio is in love with Desdemona by pointing out that Cassio slipped away from Desdemona just as Othello was approaching.]
5. Why does Othello ask Iago to watch Desdemona? [Othello has begun to doubt his wife's fidelity because of Iago's insinuations, so he wants Iago to spy on her to find out whether she is being unfaithful.]
6. What item does Emilia steal from Desdemona? [She steals the handkerchief Othello gave Desdemona.]

OBSERVATION ASSESSMENT Use the following checklist to rate each student's participation in class discussion.

3 Always   **2** Sometimes   **1** Rarely

_____ Actively participates in discussion

_____ Articulates ideas clearly

_____ Listens to what other students say

_____ Thinks before speaking

_____ Waits to be called upon

_____ Supports responses with reasons and evidence

*Drama Study Guide: **The Tragedy of Othello, the Moor of Venice***

Act IV

Strategies for Inclusion

ADVANCED After students read Act IV, have them choose a character who could, at some point, have changed what has happened. Tell students to rewrite the scene at that point, showing how things would have happened had the character acted differently.

VISUAL/AUDITORY Have students work in small groups to create a computer-animated scene with sound. Each group should choose a short portion of a scene from the play. One student might be in charge of getting information on how the technology works, another might do the artwork, another might plan the animation, while another might create the sound.

Integrating the Language Arts

WRITING: NOVEL EXCERPT Have students work singly or in small groups to translate a portion of *Othello* into an excerpt from a novel. Ask them to read their excerpts aloud, and discuss as a class how reading a novel is different from reading a play.

SPEAKING AND LISTENING Ask students to choose a **character** from *Othello*. Tell them to imagine that they will be introducing that character as the guest speaker at a banquet, and ask them to write a brief introduction. Remind them that introductions can be serious or humorous. Afterward, have students deliver their introductions in a formal manner. Encourage them to use appropriate pauses, inflection, and enunciation in delivering their speeches.

STRATEGIC READING To review and reinforce the chronology of the play, divide the class into three or four groups after everyone has finished reading Act IV. Have one student in each group read or recite a memorable or important line from the play. Ask the other students in the group to identify the speaker and the situation in which the line is spoken.

Cooperative Learning

HOT SEAT This collaborative activity allows students to pretend to become a character in literature. Have the class brainstorm to come up with a list of questions and answers. Then, divide the class into small groups of three or four students, and have each student portray one of the characters in the play. Tell students to take turns responding in character to questions posed by the other group members.

DIRECTOR FOR A DAY Divide the class into small groups, and ask them to imagine that they are directing a production of *Othello*. Have each group choose one scene and write directions for characterization, timing, blocking, costuming, and sound effects. Groups should then implement these directions by rehearsing their scenes. Finally, each group might stage its scene for the rest of the class.

Crossing the Curriculum

ART Have students work in groups of four to create a piece of scenery for the play. The design of the piece should reflect a thoughtful interpretation of its role in the play. Assign each student a leadership role: an artist (to direct the painting or drawing), a production manager (to oversee the collection of building materials), a director (to compare the details in the play to the group's rendering of the scene), and a stage manager (to decide on the placement and use of the scenery).

Assessment Tools

CHECK TEST: QUESTIONS AND ANSWERS

1. What is Othello's physical reaction to his jealousy? [He falls into an epileptic trance.]
2. How does Othello misinterpret Cassio's talk about Bianca's love for Cassio? [He thinks that Cassio is talking about Desdemona, not Bianca.]
3. What orders does Othello receive from Venice in Act IV, Scene 1? [He receives orders to return to Venice and appoint Cassio his successor in Cyprus.]
4. What does Iago urge Roderigo to do in Act IV, Scene 2? [He urges Roderigo to kill Cassio.]
5. What does Desdemona ask Emilia to do with her wedding sheets if she should die? [She asks Emilia to use the sheets as her shroud.]

OBSERVATION ASSESSMENT Use the following checklist as you observe and assess students' participation in class discussion.

3 Always   **2** Sometimes   **1** Rarely

_____ Actively participates in discussion

_____ Articulates responses clearly

_____ Listens to what other students say

_____ Thinks before speaking

_____ Waits to be called on

_____ Gives reasons for responses

*Drama Study Guide: **The Tragedy of Othello, the Moor of Venice***

Act V

Strategies for Inclusion

ENGLISH LANGUAGE DEVELOPMENT To help students stay focused on **plot,** work with them on keeping a time line of the actions that take place. Pause periodically to review what has happened in the play.

VISUAL/AUDITORY Have students work in groups of three or four to create a computer-animated scene with sound. Have each group choose a short portion of a scene from the play and use available technology to make a presentation. Suggest that one student learn how to use the equipment, another do the artwork, another plan the animation, and another create the sound.

Integrating the Language Arts

STRATEGIC READING To review the sequence of events in *Othello,* divide the class into three or four groups after everyone has finished reading the play. Have one student in each group read or recite a memorable or important line from the play, and have the other students in the group try to identify the speaker and the situation in which the line is said. Let students take turns so that everyone will have an opportunity both to read and to guess.

WRITING: NEWSPAPERS Have students work in groups of four or five to create a newspaper based on the incidents in *Othello.* Each student should contribute at least one article, and each should perform one additional task—acting as editor, typist, artist, or layout designer. Remind students to use quotations from the play in their writing. Besides articles about the major events in the play, students may want to include features such as sidebars, captioned pictures, opinion pieces or letters to the editor, classified ads, an astrological forecast, a weather report, or a travel guide.

STRATEGIC READING Assign students with different levels of ability to small groups. Have them read and raise questions about scenes from Act V. Suggest that two students read the script, one student summarize the scene, and another student write down any questions that arise. The group members should work together to use the glossary and the text to clarify understanding. Have students switch roles for each scene.

VOCABULARY To help students become familiar with Elizabethan English, ask them to find three words in the play that seem essential to understanding Shakespeare and to find two words they

believe are less frequently used. Ask for a volunteer to record the fifteen or twenty words deemed most important by students. Another list might be made of fifteen to twenty useful but not essential Elizabethan expressions. Have students write sentences with any two words from each list.

Cooperative Learning

FIELDING QUESTIONS Put up a large sheet of kraft paper, and ask students to write questions on it as they read. Tell them to leave room between questions so that other students can write in answers. Periodically check to make sure that misconceptions have been cleared up. Leave a few minutes at the beginning or the end of class to discuss the posted questions and answers and to allow students to add or answer questions.

ON-LINE GROUP PROJECTS Exchange ideas with others teaching *Othello* by posting a request on an English teaching listserv for collaborative projects.

Assessment Tools

CHECK TEST: QUESTIONS AND ANSWERS

1. Who attacks Cassio in Act V, Scene 1? [Roderigo attacks Cassio, at Iago's urging.]
2. Whom does Othello plan to murder? [He plans to murder Desdemona, for her supposed infidelity.]
3. Whom does Iago stab? [He stabs Cassio.]
4. What lie does Othello tell Desdemona in Act V, Scene 2? [He tells her that Cassio has confessed to their unlawful liaison.]
5. Why does Iago kill Emilia? [He kills her because she has exposed him as Othello's deceiver.]
6. Who kills Othello, and why? [Othello kills himself, out of remorse for murdering his innocent wife.]

INFORMAL ASSESSMENT On a scale of one to five (five points being the best), rate students' use of the play's language to respond to questions and participate in class discussions. Use the following criteria:

1 The student uses important words from the play (for example, theme words).
2 The student quotes lines from the play when appropriate.
3 The student cites lines correctly.

Plot Synopsis and Literary Focus

Act I

Scene 1 Iago complains bitterly to Roderigo, a Venetian gentleman, that Othello, the leading military figure in Venice, has chosen Cassio to be his lieutenant, or second in command. Iago is convinced that he is the better soldier and deeply resents what he sees as Othello's unfair preference for Cassio. He tells Roderigo that he will continue to pose as Othello's loyal follower but will secretly be acting to further his own interests. The pair rush to the house of Brabantio, a Venetian senator, to tell him that his daughter, Desdemona, has just eloped with Othello. Roderigo, who had wanted to marry Desdemona, enjoys giving Brabantio, who had rejected him as a suitor for his daughter, the bad news that Desdemona has married without her father's permission.

Literary Focus In the first scene we are given insight into Iago's **motives** and his plan of action. He is angry and jealous, and his ambition has been thwarted by Cassio's promotion. He plans to play the hypocrite, seeming to be loyal but secretly plotting vengeance: "I am not what I am" (line 63). This **theme** of appearance versus reality will recur throughout the play.

Scene 2 Iago goes to the place where Othello and Desdemona are spending their wedding night and tells Othello that Brabantio is angry about the marriage, pretending to be concerned for Othello's safety. Othello expresses his love for Desdemona and his confidence that because of his personal virtues and military value to the state, the duke of Venice and his nobles will not turn against him. Cassio arrives with an urgent summons for Othello from the duke. Venice's enemies, the Turks, appear to be heading for Venetian-controlled Cyprus. Next, Brabantio and Roderigo arrive. Brabantio calls for Othello's arrest, accusing him of stealing Brabantio's innocent daughter by trickery or enchantment. Othello says he is willing to answer any charges against him, but then he suggests that the emergency facing the state is more urgent than these domestic conflicts.

Literary Focus The **characterization** of Iago as a hypocrite continues with his pretense of wanting to harm Brabantio for Othello's sake after having said that he could not contemplate violence outside war. The **ironic contrast** between appearance and reality recurs when Iago and Roderigo present themselves as opponents although they are really confidants united in their enmity toward Othello.

Scene 3 The duke and the senators are trying to sort out confusing reports about the movements of the Turkish fleet when Brabantio and Othello enter, accompanied by Iago and Roderigo. Brabantio tells the duke that Othello must have cast a spell on his daughter, for a modest and obedient girl like Desdemona would never freely marry a man like Othello. The duke declares that he needs more proof than Brabantio's account of his daughter's character and asks Othello for his version of the marriage. Othello suggests that Desdemona herself be questioned. She is sent for, and while waiting for her, Othello explains that as a guest in Brabantio's home he recounted his wide-ranging adventures as a soldier, and Desdemona listened with great interest: "She loved me for the dangers I had passed, / And I loved her that she did pity them" (lines 166–167). When Desdemona appears, she addresses her father respectfully, but unequivocally professes her loyalty and devotion to Othello. Reluctantly Brabantio accepts what he cannot alter.

Arrangements must be made for Desdemona since the welfare of Venice requires that Othello leave for Cyprus immediately. Desdemona requests that she be allowed to accompany her husband, and Othello agrees in order to please her, he says, not to satisfy his personal desires. Desdemona is left in the temporary care of Iago, whom Othello believes to be honest.

Finally, Iago and Roderigo are alone on the stage, and Roderigo, disappointed and jealous because he has lost Desdemona, threatens to drown himself. Iago mocks Roderigo's willingness to end his life on account of disappointed love and cynically advises him to raise cash and wait patiently for another chance to get what he wants. Alone, Iago hatches a plan to ruin Othello. He will slyly suggest to the Moor that the handsome Cassio is secretly seeing Desdemona.

Literary Focus The **exposition** of the **conflicts** that drive the play expands in this scene, as does the exploration of Othello's character and that of his **antagonist,** Iago. The major conflicts are both interpersonal and internal. Brabantio suspects Othello of sorcery and rejects him because of his race. Iago and Roderigo are motivated by hatred and jealousy of Othello. Othello presents himself as a simple man who has spent his life in military service. His fatal flaw, according to the critic

Drama Study Guide: The Tragedy of Othello, the Moor of Venice

HRW MATERIAL COPYRIGHTED UNDER NOTICE APPEARING EARLIER IN THIS WORK.

27

G. B. Harrison, is his belief that others are what they seem. Othello's status as a **tragic hero** (a good person who suffers because of a weakness) is foreshadowed in Brabantio's suspicious warning: "Look to her, Moor, if thou hast eyes to see: / She has deceived her father, and may thee" (lines 288–289).

In his dialogue with Roderigo and in the closing **soliloquy,** Iago is revealed as a calculating and sly cynic whose only passion is for revenge. In the **extended metaphor** of the body as a garden (lines 316–322), Iago extols the supremacy of willpower over all human emotions.

Act II

Scene 1 In the midst of a fierce storm, Montano, the governor of Cyprus, and other gentlemen stand on the shore, awaiting news of the Turkish fleet. They are informed that a Venetian ship has entered the harbor with a report that the Turkish ships have been destroyed at sea and Othello's ship was lost sight of in the gale. Cassio then enters and tells of Othello's marriage to Desdemona. Soon the ship carrying Desdemona, Iago, and his wife, Emilia, arrives, and those three come onstage. Cassio greets Desdemona with gallant praises. She thanks him cursorily and expresses her concern for Othello's safety. Immediately another ship, presumably Othello's, is sighted. Cassio greets Emilia with a kiss, and Iago engages in some clever but meanspirited commentary on his wife's open nature and on women in general. At first, Desdemona humors Iago, but finally she is put off by his cynical wit. When the courtly Cassio kisses Desdemona's hand, Iago, in an aside, vows, "With as little a web as this will I ensnare as great a fly as Cassio" (lines 166–167). Othello then arrives, and he and Desdemona have an impassioned reunion, which inflames Iago's desire for revenge.

Left alone with Roderigo, Iago sets his plan in motion by convincing Roderigo that Desdemona is in love with Cassio. In a long prose speech, Iago stokes Roderigo's jealousy by portraying Desdemona as tired of the older Othello and captivated by the younger, handsomer Cassio. He paints Cassio as a zealous opportunist and asks Roderigo to provoke Cassio's anger, assuring him that by doing so he will win Desdemona. Alone, Iago mulls over his own feelings and motives. He admires Othello but hates him, perhaps because of Othello's virtuous nature. Iago says that he, too, loves Desdemona, but more out of vengefulness than desire.

Literary Focus The scene continues to characterize Iago as a clever, hypocritical villain. Iago puts on a false face to all, pretending to be the loyal servant of Othello and Desdemona while secretly plotting to destroy their happiness. He even manipulates his confederate, Roderigo. In his scene-ending soliloquy the audience gets a direct view of Iago's twisted soul, which seems to take pleasure in giving pain. Many critics, including Samuel Taylor Coleridge and Bernard Spivack, have seen Iago's plotting as "motiveless malignity" and consider his dramatic role as evil incarnate to be an outgrowth of the Vice figure in medieval morality plays.

Iago's **foil** Cassio is all flattery and grand manners. He praises women, particularly the fair Desdemona, as extravagantly as Iago belittles them. Unlike the introspective Iago, the sunny Cassio has little insight into his own or others' motives.

Scene 2 A herald, or messenger, reads a proclamation to the people of Cyprus from Othello. It announces that a festival will be held that evening to celebrate the destruction of the Turkish fleet and the wedding of Othello. Food and drink are to be provided, and all are invited to enjoy themselves.

Literary Focus During this brief scene both leader and people are given permission to enjoy the fruits of good fortune. The public and private domains are in harmony, and there is a pause in the movement of Iago's plan to undermine Othello's happiness.

Scene 3 Othello, in Desdemona's presence, asks Cassio to be sure the celebrations do not get out of hand. He and Desdemona then leave, and Iago enters and engages Cassio in conversation. Cassio admits that he cannot tolerate liquor yet gives in to Iago's urging to drink with Montano and some of the other Cypriots. Cassio departs drunkenly, and Iago suggests to Montano that the lieutenant is often unfit for duty. At Iago's prodding, Cassio gets into a fight with Roderigo. Montano, shocked by the brawling, intervenes and is wounded by Cassio just as Othello arrives to find out the cause of the commotion, which has disturbed his private hours with Desdemona and the peace of the island. Iago, instigator of the entire incident, pretends to be innocent of its cause and desirous of protecting Cassio. Giving way to anger for the first time, Othello strips Cassio of his rank as lieutenant.

Alone with Iago, a remorseful Cassio laments the loss of his good name, "the immortal part of

Drama Study Guide: The Tragedy of Othello, the Moor of Venice

myself" (lines 257–258). Pretending to be sympathetic and helpful, Iago suggests that Cassio seek Desdemona's aid in getting his position back: "This broken joint between you and her husband entreat her to splinter" (lines 315–316). When alone, Iago takes delight in the destruction he is engineering, associating himself with images of hell.

> . . . Divinity of hell!
> When devils will the blackest sins put on,
> They do suggest at first with heavenly shows,
> As I do now.
>
> —lines 341–343

The scene ends with Roderigo declaring that he will return to Venice and Iago persuading him to stay.

Literary Focus This scene reveals further weaknesses in the essentially good characters of Othello and Cassio. Like Othello, Cassio is credulous and easily led by the crafty Iago. Cassio, too, seems unable to distinguish the appearance of friendship from the reality. Although he is aware of his inability to tolerate alcohol, he gives in to Iago's urging to take a drink. Othello, who knows the need to control his temper, allows himself to fly into a rage when he sees that his lieutenant, whom he charged with keeping the peace, is the person most responsible for disturbing it.

Iago, in this scene, is portrayed as an evil, predatory figure. He uses images of hunting and trapping to describe himself, taking pleasure, for example, in making "the net / That shall enmesh them all" (lines 352–353).

Act III

Scene 1   The next day, in front of the castle where Othello and Desdemona are staying, Cassio pays some musicians to play something and greet Othello. A clown in Othello's service then enters, comically insults the musicians, pays them not to play, and dismisses them. Cassio asks the clown to fetch Emilia, Iago's wife. The clown leaves, Iago enters, and Cassio tells him of his plan to gain access to Desdemona through Emilia. The ever-helpful Iago offers to further Cassio's plan by drawing Othello away so that Cassio can unburden himself to Desdemona in private. Emilia tells Cassio that Desdemona has already spoken to Othello on his behalf and that the general's anger has cooled and he is looking for a way to reinstate Cassio without offending the citizens of Cyprus, who are upset by Cassio's having wounded the respected Montano. Emilia promises to help Cassio speak privately with Desdemona.

Literary Focus   After the brief **comic relief** supplied by the clown and the musicians, the play refocuses on the sinister **main plot** of deceit and destruction. Cassio, now Iago's complete dupe, exclaims that even the residents of his hometown are not "more kind and honest" than Iago (line 37). (This ironic linking of the word *honest* with Iago is repeated throughout the play.) Emilia, too, is ignorant of her husband's schemes and genuinely wishes to help the distraught Cassio. Othello is busy with his professional duties, and this enables Iago to further his malicious plans.

Scene 2   In this brief scene, Othello carries out his professional duties; he gives Iago letters to send to the senators in Venice and leaves to view some fortifications with the local gentlemen.

Scene 3   In the garden of the castle, Desdemona, in Emilia's presence, confidently assures Cassio that she will reconcile him and her husband. When Cassio sees Othello and Iago approaching, he leaves quickly. Iago uses this opportunity to plant the first seed of suspicion in Othello's mind:

> . . . No, sure, I cannot think it,
> That he would steal away so guilty-like,
> Seeing you coming.
>
> —lines 38–40

Desdemona immediately presses Othello to recall Cassio. Confused by her persistence, Othello says that he will grant her request but asks her not to press him any further at present. When she leaves, he professes both love and fear: "But I do love thee! and when I love thee not, / Chaos is come again" (lines 91–92). Now Iago embarks on undermining Othello's trust in Desdemona, all the while seeming reluctant to speak and therefore in possession of some truly damning knowledge of the relationship between Desdemona and Cassio. Finally, in a moment of great irony, Iago, who is fostering Othello's jealousy, warns:

> O, beware, my lord, of jealousy!
> It is the green-eyed monster which doth mock
> The meat it feeds on.
>
> —lines 165–167

*Drama Study Guide: **The Tragedy of Othello, the Moor of Venice***

Othello is thrown into a state of doubt and anxiety. Iago piles one insinuation upon another, suggesting that because Desdemona deceived her father, she might also fool Othello. Torn now between love and doubt, Othello asks Iago to watch Desdemona, to see whether she acts suspiciously. To himself he exclaims, "If she be false, heaven mocks itself! / I'll not believe't" (lines 277–278).

Now Desdemona and Emilia return. Hearing that Othello has a headache, Desdemona offers to soothe his head by wrapping it with her handkerchief. He pushes the handkerchief aside, and it falls to the floor. They leave, and Emilia, recognizing Othello's first and much cherished gift to Desdemona, which Iago has been urging his wife to steal, picks it up. Not knowing why her husband wants the handkerchief but wishing to please him, Emilia gives it to Iago when he reenters. She then exits.

Othello now returns, mad with jealousy, and demands that Iago give him proof of Desdemona's guilt. Iago, seemingly with reluctance, tells how he recently spent a night with Cassio and heard him, while he slept, professing his passion for Desdemona. Then Iago tells Othello that he saw Cassio using the handkerchief Othello had given Desdemona. This last piece of circumstantial evidence convinces Othello, and he vows never to rest until his wife and Cassio are punished. Iago offers his services, and Othello accepts, asking him to kill Cassio within three days. Iago then pleads with Othello to spare Desdemona's life and vows his allegiance to him.

Literary Focus This scene, in which Iago labors to convince Othello of the guilt of the innocent Desdemona, is the **turning point** of the play. Countless critics have asked how a man as noble as Othello, who clearly loves his wife, could be convinced of her infidelity on the slight circumstantial evidence offered by just one man. Many point out that Othello's reaction to Iago's deception is not surprising since everyone in the play believes Iago to be honest, and everyone, including his own wife and his apparent ally, Roderigo, is deceived by him. Others support Othello's behavior by pointing to the brevity of his marriage, which has not given him time to get to know his wife. Still others point to his being a lifelong soldier and a foreigner—the former kept him from understanding women; the latter, from understanding the ways of a society as sophisticated as that of Venice. These critics say that Othello was aware of his weaknesses, and because of them, and because of his race and his age, he was insecure about his relationship with Desdemona. Such critics as Paul A. Jorgensen have reasoned that Othello

was unused to happiness and therefore afraid of it. According to Jorgensen, "Iago's strategy . . . is to unsettle whatever glimpses of happiness Othello may have, [and] to play on his imagined difficulties and insecurities."

Othello's discourse in this scene veers from the noble to the bestial, the latter when he is in the grip of jealousy and murderous rage. Critics like Robert Heilman and Carolyn Spurgeon point out that as Othello falls under Iago's poisonous influence, he begins to use language that was earlier associated with Iago. This is especially evident in his final speech in this scene:

> . . . Damn her, lewd minx! O damn her! Damn her!
> Come, go with me apart. I will withdraw
> To furnish me with some swift means of death
> For the fair devil.
> —lines 472–475

Scene 4 Desdemona, in Emilia's presence, asks the clown to bring Cassio to the castle, for she believes she has persuaded Othello to reinstate his lieutenant. The clown indulges in some punning before going off to fetch Cassio. Desdemona then enlists Emilia's help in finding the lost handkerchief. Emilia, lying, says she knows nothing of it. When Emilia asks whether Othello is jealous, Desdemona confidently asserts that he is not. Othello then enters, determined to test Desdemona's honesty. She interrupts him with a reminder of his promise to recall Cassio, unwittingly increasing his jealous fears. Instead of replying, Othello asks her for the handkerchief. His speech places so much significance on the gift as a token of love and fidelity that Desdemona lies, saying it is not lost, and quickly returns to her pleas for Cassio. Othello again asks her to get the handkerchief, she refuses, and he storms off, leaving Desdemona perplexed and amazed and Emilia convinced of his jealousy.

Iago and Cassio enter together. At Iago's urging, Cassio renews his pleas to Desdemona, and she replies, "What I can do I will; and more I will / Than for myself I dare" (lines 131–132). Iago offers to find out what is bothering Othello, and Desdemona accepts.

All but Cassio leave, and Bianca enters. She chides Cassio for his recent absence from her. He speaks lovingly to her and gives her a handkerchief that he admits he recently found in his room (where Iago planted it). She becomes jealous, suspecting that Cassio got the handkerchief from another woman.

Literary Focus This scene highlights two central themes of the play: deceit and jealousy. We

Drama Study Guide: The Tragedy of Othello, the Moor of Venice

have become used to the chronic and conscious lying and manipulation by Iago, the play's unsympathetic character. Now, however, the sympathetic characters also lie or deceive themselves or others, though generally they are less conscious of their behavior than Iago is of his. First Emilia lies about the handkerchief to Desdemona, presumably to protect Iago, and then Desdemona, in a fatal error, lies about it to Othello. Desdemona may be deceiving herself about her husband's nature and the degree of influence she has over him, or she may simply lack the experience to know him and herself better.

Bianca's jealousy mirrors Othello's; it is incited by flimsy circumstantial evidence and is perhaps rooted in a similar lack of self-confidence and insecurity. In lines 161–162, Emilia reprises the monster imagery that Iago used earlier to characterize jealousy: "It is a monster / Begot upon itself, born on itself."

Act IV

Scene 1 Iago has now become the complete master of Othello, inflaming his jealousy with ever more graphic insinuations about the supposed intimacy between Desdemona and Cassio. Othello's rage makes him fall into an epileptic trance, during which Cassio enters. Iago instructs Cassio to leave and return after Othello has recovered and departed. When Othello comes to, Iago tells him that he is expecting Cassio and instructs him to stand a little way off in order to observe Cassio's happy demeanor as he talks about Desdemona. When Cassio returns, Iago leads him to talk lightheartedly about Bianca's love for him. Completely irrational now, Othello readily interprets as incriminating evidence what he sees but cannot hear. Then Bianca arrives and angrily returns the handkerchief to Cassio, convinced that it belongs to a rival. A maddened Othello emerges once Bianca and Cassio have left. To Othello the handkerchief in the hands of Bianca seals the case against Cassio and Desdemona. He alternately threatens to kill them both and raves about Desdemona's gentle charms. Iago advises Othello to strangle Desdemona in the same bed in which she supposedly betrayed him and offers to take care of Cassio himself.

Lodovico then arrives from Venice with letters ordering Othello to return and appointing Cassio his successor in Cyprus. When Desdemona expresses pleasure at this news, Othello strikes her and then taunts her. Lodovico is greatly shocked and marvels that he could have been so mistaken in his appraisal of Othello's character.

Literary Focus In this scene the previously disciplined Othello loses both his rationality and his humanity and descends to the level of an unreasoning beast. Iago, the man who is responsible for driving Othello mad, dares tell him to "be a man" (line 66). Lacking Iago's coldness, Othello is mad with jealousy because he still loves Desdemona even though he believes she has wronged him. His conflicting emotions are reflected in speeches that are full of **paradox,** or contradiction, like this one: "Ay, let her rot, and perish, and be damned. . . . O, the world hath not a sweeter creature!" (lines 179–182).

Egged on by Iago, the brute in Othello now has the upper hand. This is demonstrated when he exclaims "I will chop her into messes!" (line 197) and when, in response to Iago's suggestion that he kill his wife in her bed, he says "The justice of it pleases" (line 206).

Scene 2 Othello interrogates Emilia about his wife's fidelity but dismisses her sworn avowals of Desdemona's purity. Emilia suspects that some wicked person has misled Othello and, not knowing that her husband is that person, calls for the worst of curses on the guilty party. After speaking to Emilia as if she were a servant in a brothel, Othello bitterly confronts Desdemona. She senses his anger and protests her innocence but has no idea what she is being accused of. Othello, hoping to damn her in the next life, makes her swear that she is honest. Then he gives way to self-pity, claiming that he could have withstood any misfortune but this one, since he had made his love for her the center of his life. Calling her a whore and again speaking cruelly to Emilia, he storms out. Devastated, Desdemona asks Emilia to put the couple's wedding sheets on their bed and to summon Iago. In response to Desdemona's request that he tell her how to win Othello back, Iago belittles her troubles.

After leaving the two women, Iago encounters Roderigo, who reveals that he has given Iago jewels to give to Desdemona and is tired of waiting for her favors in return. Iago persuades him to wait just one more night for the satisfaction of his desires and urges him to kill Cassio in order to prevent the departure of Othello and Desdemona.

Literary Focus This scene is notable for its **dramatic irony** and disturbing **pathos.** Only the

*Drama Study Guide: **The Tragedy of Othello, the Moor of Venice***

HRW MATERIAL COPYRIGHTED UNDER NOTICE APPEARING EARLIER IN THIS WORK.

31

audience and the diabolical Iago understand everything that is happening. Othello, in a blind rage, is wounding and besmirching what he loves most. Desdemona is accused of a crime she never even contemplated. And Emilia, who calls for hideous curses to be brought down on the person responsible for Othello's behavior, unwittingly damns her own husband. Desdemona's helpless innocence and her pathetic turn to Iago for advice not only sadden the audience but also move viewers to join Emilia in her desire to see avenged the villain who has brought these two worthy, if flawed, lovers to such a sorry state.

Scene 3 Upon bidding good night to Lodovico, Othello orders Desdemona to go to her bedroom, dismiss her servant, and wait for him. Desdemona, eager to pacify the angry Othello, returns to her room and asks Emilia to help her undress and then to leave her. When Emilia criticizes Othello, Desdemona defends him but then, in what is undoubtedly an unconscious premonition, asks Emilia to use her wedding sheets as a shroud if she should die. Desdemona sings a melancholy song

about lost love, then asks Emilia whether many women betray their husbands and whether she would ever do so. Emilia, older, more worldly, and more pragmatic than Desdemona, declares that she would be unfaithful if the reward were great enough. Emilia then decries the double standard that permits men, but not their wives, to stray, even when the wives have been given much cause to do so.

Literary Focus This intimate scene, which takes place almost entirely in Desdemona's bedroom and consists mostly of conversation between the two women, underscores the domestic nature of the play's conflict. The women talk of marital fidelity and of the relations between husbands and wives. Desdemona, idealistic and naive, seems almost unable to conceive of infidelity. The more realistic Emilia serves as her foil. Some critics have questioned the credibility of Desdemona's character. Could a young noblewoman from a society as sophisticated and decadent as that of sixteenth-century Venice be so unworldly and so inept at protecting herself from a jealous husband?

Act V

Scene 1 On a street near Bianca's house, Iago sets Roderigo up to attack Cassio when he passes. In an aside, Iago reveals that he would not mind seeing both men dead, since either could expose him. When Cassio enters, Roderigo strikes at him with a sword but misses; Cassio retaliates and wounds Roderigo. Iago stabs Cassio in the leg from behind and leaves unseen. Othello hears Cassio's cries for help and assumes that Iago has attacked him as he had promised. Othello takes this act as a sign of Iago's friendship and is emboldened by it to carry out his own plan to murder Desdemona.

After Othello leaves the scene, the Venetian visitors Lodovico and Gratiano come along and hear the groans of the wounded but are afraid to investigate on their own. Then Iago comes forth carrying a lantern and weapons. Cassio recognizes his voice and asks for help. Iago takes advantage of the confusion to stab Roderigo while pretending he is defending Cassio from an unknown ruffian. Always the hypocrite, Iago offers his shirt to bind Cassio's wounded leg. Bianca then enters. When Gratiano realizes that the man Iago stabbed is Roderigo, Iago suggests that Bianca is to blame. Emilia enters, and Iago explains the fight as "the fruits of whoring" (line 117) and instructs his wife to tell Othello and Desdemona what has happened.

Literary Focus Now the play moves from vicious words to violent acts. True to his furtive nature, Iago stabs a man under the cover of night and then pretends to be a friend and rescuer. The other characters, except the dying Roderigo, remain in the dark regarding Iago's true nature. Roderigo's words—"O damned Iago! O inhuman dog!" (line 62)—echo the animal imagery that has been associated with Iago throughout the play. Iago himself heightens the **dramatic tension** with his recognition, in the final lines of the scene, that this bloody night's deeds, which he has instigated, will make or doom him.

Scene 2 Othello enters the room where his wife sleeps, speaks of how he shall kill her, then kisses her. Desdemona awakens, and he instructs her to pray, to confess "any crime / Unreconciled as yet to heaven and grace" (lines 26–27). Unwilling to believe his wife's avowals of innocence, Othello claims that Cassio has confessed to their unlawful liaison. When she asks that Cassio be sent for, Othello admits that the man has been killed. Desdemona pleads for her life, but her husband replies, "Being done, there is no pause" (line 82), and he smothers her.

Emilia calls from outside, and Othello, not sure whether Desdemona is still alive, closes the bed curtains and lets Emilia in. Emilia reports that Roderigo is dead and Cassio wounded. Desdemona then cries out that she has been murdered and is dying. Emilia asks her mistress, "Who hath done this deed?" (line 123), and with her last words, Desdemona claims to have killed herself. After hesitating, Othello admits that he has killed his wife, and Emilia responds, "O the more angel she, / And you the blacker devil!" (lines 130–131).

Upon learning from Othello that it was Iago's testimony that convinced him of Desdemona's guilt, Emilia brands her husband's soul "pernicious" (line 155). As Othello threatens her, Emilia calls out that he has murdered Desdemona.

Montano, Gratiano, and Iago then arrive and learn that Desdemona has been murdered. Gratiano tells them that Brabantio has died of a broken heart; Desdemona's "match was mortal to him" (line 205). Emilia confronts Iago and will not be silenced until his villainy and Desdemona's innocence are clear to all. When Othello finally perceives Iago's treachery, he moves to attack his former ally but is disarmed by Montano. Iago then stabs Emilia. Mortally wounded, she asks to be laid beside the body of her beloved mistress. Iago runs out, and Montano goes after him, leaving Gratiano to stand guard outside the room. Othello, now alone, finds a sword and determines to kill himself, but not before trying to explain his actions to Gratiano, whom he calls into the room. Montano then returns with Lodovico, Cassio, and Iago, who is now a prisoner. Othello wounds Iago and is again disarmed. Finally, all Iago's machinations are revealed. Lodovico moves to take Othello back to Venice, where his fate will be decided. Othello admits his errors, then stabs himself and dies. Lodovico leaves Cassio to deal with Iago and ends the play by stating "Myself will straight aboard, and to the state / This heavy act with heavy heart relate" (lines 369–370).

Literary Focus The tragic **denouement** begins with Desdemona's murder, which has qualities of a love scene, since Othello kisses his wife before he kills her. (The kiss also recalls Judas's betrayal of Jesus.) The language of the scene reflects other oppositions that have been present throughout the play, such as fairness versus darkness, knowledge versus ignorance, and appearance versus reality. Othello kills the person he loves most and sees dishonesty where there is none, yet in the end even Cassio calls him "great of heart" (line 360). The restoration of order and the administration of justice are left to Cassio and the other gentlemen, who blame Iago—"O Spartan dog!" (line 360)—for all the bloodshed, but the audience is left to ponder the degree to which Othello is responsible for his own downfall.

Drama Study Guide: The Tragedy of Othello, the Moor of Venice

HRW MATERIAL COPYRIGHTED UNDER NOTICE APPEARING EARLIER IN THIS WORK.

33

Guided Reading

The questions and comments that follow focus on the staging, characterization, and plot development of the play. They ask students for opinions and comments and are designed to help them think about and respond to the play as they read it. The questions correspond to specific lines in the play and are followed by answers or sample responses. You may want to use these questions and comments to help students who are having difficulty with the play; they can provide an opportunity to stop and catch up on the plot or understand the thinking of a particular character.

Act I   Scene 1

LINE 16. *The play opens with a dialogue between Iago and Roderigo about an unnamed third person. What is the tone of their exchange? If you were directing the play, how would you advise the two actors to deliver their lines?*

ANSWER. The exchange is quarrelsome. Roderigo might speak in a whiny, aggrieved voice, and Iago might respond with weary patience, giving good reasons for his hostile feelings toward the unnamed third person.

LINE 25. *What feelings is Iago expressing toward Cassio in this speech? What gesture or body movement might help reveal his feelings?*

ANSWER. Iago is expressing envy, anger, and a sense of superiority. He might wave his hand to show dismissal or disgust when pronouncing "Mere prattle, without practice" (line 24).

LINE 31. *This is the first time that Iago has referred to the person he is angry with by any term other than the pronoun* he. *What does his use of the phrase* his Moorship *suggest about his feelings toward Othello, his commanding officer?*

ANSWER. Iago's word choice suggests contempt for Othello and resentment of his authority.

LINE 38. *In what sense does Roderigo use the word* follow *here? Note how Iago takes up the word and uses it in a variety of contexts in his response to Roderigo.*

ANSWER. Roderigo means *follow* in the sense of "to take orders from" or "to be subordinate to."

LINE 63. *How would you have Iago deliver this speech, in which he reveals how he plans to present himself to Othello?*

ANSWER. Iago might speak in a low, conspiratorial tone of voice, since he is confiding his secret strategy. Or he might display a sense of self-satisfied pride in the cunning of his plan to deceive Othello.

LINE 72. *What does "Here is her father's house" suggest that Iago and Roderigo have been doing while speaking the preceding lines?*

ANSWER. It suggests that they have been walking toward Brabantio's house.

LINE 79. *In what tone of voice would you have Iago deliver this speech?*

ANSWER. Iago might speak in a loud, urgent tone designed to frighten and alarm the sleeping Brabantio.

AFTER LINE 79, STAGE DIRECTION. *How would you have Brabantio appear when he comes to the window?*

ANSWER. Brabantio should be dressed in sleeping attire and appear disheveled and disoriented, as one would be when suddenly aroused from sleep.

LINE 87. *Note the animal imagery and the references to blackness that Iago uses when referring to Othello. What attitudes in Brabantio is Iago appealing to? Look for similar imagery as the play proceeds.*

ANSWER. Iago is appealing to Brabantio's color prejudice and to his sense that a possession (his daughter) has been wrongfully taken from him.

LINE 99. *What attitude toward Roderigo does Brabantio take when he first recognizes him?*

ANSWER. Brabantio assumes that Roderigo is drunk and is making trouble because he was not permitted to marry Desdemona.

*Drama Study Guide: **The Tragedy of Othello, the Moor of Venice***

LINE 105. *What are members of the audience expected to feel when Roderigo speaks this line?*

ANSWER. They are expected to appreciate the irony in Roderigo's words, since there is nothing "pure" in his coming to see Brabantio; he is there for revenge.

LINE 134. *How does Roderigo characterize Othello in these lines? Keep his words in mind when Othello appears later in the act, and decide whether there is any truth in this characterization.*

ANSWER. Roderigo characterizes Othello as an exotic and boastful outsider of unknown origins.

LINE 138. *This is the first of many instances in the play when a character calls for light. Such remarks helped Shakespeare's audiences follow the time of day in which the action was taking place, since there were no electrical lights to dim or turn up to indicate night or day. What symbolic meaning might Brabantio's call for light have?*

ANSWER. Brabantio's demand might symbolize his desire to dispel his fears about his daughter or his hope of getting a clearer understanding of her situation.

LINE 171. *How has Brabantio's tone toward Roderigo changed in this speech?*

ANSWER. Brabantio has been chastened by the news of his daughter and Othello. He now adopts a worried, pleading tone with Roderigo, looking for reassurance from the man he previously dismissed.

LINE 180. *With what gesture might Brabantio accompany these words?*

ANSWER. He might hold his head, wring his hands, or clutch his heart.

Scene 2

BEFORE LINE 1, STAGE DIRECTION. *What is indicated by the fact that the attendants are carrying torches?*

ANSWER. It is still night.

LINE 5. *Iago claims here to lack the evil will needed to strike Brabantio, Othello's accuser. How would you have him deliver this blatantly ironic speech?*

ANSWER. Most contemporary actors play Iago as if he meant every word he says, since that is how

he wishes to appear and how all the other characters see him. Earlier actors sometimes allowed him a wicked sneer or an evil grin when unobserved by the other characters.

LINE 27. *In this speech, Othello expresses confidence that his personal qualities and history of service to the state will silence any criticism of him. When he speaks of Desdemona, would you have him change his tone of voice?*

ANSWER. Othello might continue speaking calmly and confidently, or he might switch to a more tender or a more fervent tone when he speaks of his great love for Desdemona.

LINE 32. *What physical interaction might occur between Iago and Othello as the men with torches approach from offstage?*

ANSWER. Iago might attempt to guide or point Othello indoors; Othello might push Iago aside or ignore his gesture and move boldly upstage toward the men.

LINE 46. *Given the content of Cassio's message, at what pace would you have him deliver it?*

ANSWER. Since Cassio has an urgent summons for Othello from the duke and presumably has been rushing around looking for Othello, he would probably speak quickly and breathlessly.

LINE 48. *Why do you think Othello goes back into the house after speaking with Cassio?*

ANSWER. He undoubtedly goes to tell Desdemona that he has been summoned by the duke.

AFTER LINE 53, STAGE DIRECTION. *Notice that the officers with Brabantio come onstage with weapons. What does this tell you about Brabantio's mood and intentions?*

ANSWER. Brabantio is very angry and is willing to use violence to apprehend Othello, whom he now views as a criminal.

LINE 60. *Besides the officers on both sides, who probably draws a sword in this scene?*

ANSWER. In line 57, Iago appears to challenge Roderigo and probably draws his sword while speaking.

LINE 60. *How does Othello's manner contrast with that of the other characters when he delivers this speech?*

ANSWER. Unlike the others, Othello is calm and does not resort to threats or violence.

*Drama Study Guide: **The Tragedy of Othello, the Moor of Venice***

LINE 74. *In this long speech, what does Brabantio accuse Othello of doing?*

ANSWER. Brabantio accuses Othello of enchanting Desdemona by means of magic charms or potions.

LINE 80. *Would you direct any of Brabantio's men to lay hands on Othello?*

ANSWER. There is no stage direction calling for such action, and Othello, conscious of his dignity, would probably have protested if any of the men had moved toward him.

LINE 84. *How does Othello respond to Brabantio's charges?*

ANSWER. Othello remains calm and volunteers to answer the charges verbally.

LINE 98. *If you were directing Scene 2, how would you want the audience to feel toward Brabantio as the scene ends?*

ANSWER. A director might want the audience to feel sympathetic toward Brabantio, who has lost his daughter under circumstances he doesn't understand. Or a director might want the audience to feel pity for a foolish man who made wild accusations before knowing the facts.

Scene 3

BEFORE LINE 1, STAGE DIRECTION. *Shakespeare provides no instructions on how to position the characters onstage, how they should be costumed, or how props, other than a table, should be used. How would you arrange the duke and the senators around the table, and how would you costume them? Would you add props or scenery?*

ANSWER. As the head of state, the duke should be distinguished from the senators by the prominence of his position at the table and by his costume. Perhaps he should sit in the center and wear a badge of his rank, such as a distinctive headdress or medallion. If a director is aiming for historical accuracy, he or she can study portraits of sixteenth-century Venetian heads of state. The duke and the senators may be clad in costumes from another period, however, as long as their relative rank and wealth are reflected. Historically, *Othello* has been played with a minimum of props and scenery.

LINE 17. *What is the duke asking about here?*

ANSWER. The duke is asking for the senators' evaluation of the conflicting information he has been given about the movements of the Turkish fleet. First he was told that it was heading for Cyprus and then that it was making for Rhodes.

LINE 30. *What is the first senator's explanation of the conflicting reports?*

ANSWER. The first senator believes that the Turks are deliberately trying to trick the Venetians into thinking they are heading for Rhodes when Cyprus is their true target.

AFTER LINE 49, STAGE DIRECTION. *Would you have the duke change his tone of voice or manner when he turns from Othello to address Brabantio?*

ANSWER. At this point the duke might address each man with equal respect, since he has no reason to do otherwise. Since he urgently needs Othello's military services right now, however, the duke might greet Othello more enthusiastically than Brabantio, whose services are not crucial at the moment.

LINE 70. *Why is the duke's speech an example of dramatic irony?*

ANSWER. The speech is an example of dramatic irony because the audience knows (and the duke doesn't) that the person Brabantio is accusing and the duke is promising to punish is Othello, the very man the duke needs to defend Venice.

LINE 74. *With what emotion would you have the duke say this short line?*

ANSWER. The duke might say this line with great surprise, disappointment, or concern.

LINE 89. *Here Othello characterizes his use of language. How does he evaluate his powers of expression? As you continue to read, make your own evaluation of Othello's language.*

ANSWER. Othello believes that he can speak effectively only about military matters, that his plain speech is not suitable for expressing ideas and feelings unconnected with war.

LINE 94. *Critics have disagreed on Othello's intention in this speech. Why, in your opinion, does he present himself humbly?*

ANSWER. He may be consciously displaying a modesty he doesn't feel in order to impress his audience. Or he may be truly unaware of his power to influence others with his words.

LINE 106. *How does Brabantio see his daughter?*

ANSWER. Brabantio describes Desdemona as a shy, compliant daughter who, if not somehow charmed, would be repulsed by or afraid of Othello.

LINE 109. *The duke suggests that Brabantio prove the charges he has made against*

Drama Study Guide: The Tragedy of Othello, the Moor of Venice

36   HRW MATERIAL COPYRIGHTED UNDER NOTICE APPEARING EARLIER IN THIS WORK.

Othello. On what has Brabantio based his accusations? As the play proceeds, look for other examples of charges made, proofs demanded, and evidence provided.

ANSWER. Brabantio has based his charges on his own fears, prejudices, and assumptions about Othello and Desdemona.

LINE 120. *In this speech, how does Othello respond to Brabantio's accusations?*

ANSWER. Othello responds confidently, suggesting that Desdemona be asked whether he has done her any harm and pledging to give up his office and his life if she says he has.

LINE 121. *What does Othello's sending Iago to get Desdemona suggest about the relationship between the general and his servant?*

ANSWER. It suggests that Othello trusts Iago in domestic as well as military matters.

LINE 145. *Othello's references to "Cannibals" and "Anthropophagi" reflect Elizabethans' ideas about exotic, far-off countries. They got their information from contemporary geographies and natural histories that were more fanciful than factual. Some modern directors cut these lines. Would you?*

ANSWER. Some students may argue that these lines add to the foreignness of Othello as a character and are not out of place in the context of the time in which the play is set. Others may hold that because audiences may not understand the historical context, these lines can mistakenly be taken as evidence of Othello's ignorance and so should be cut.

LINE 170. *What is the duke's response to Othello's account of his wooing of Desdemona? How does this reflect on Othello's way with words?*

ANSWER. The duke finds Othello's account convincing. This suggests that others find Othello's oratory persuasive despite his own modesty about it.

LINE 178. *What answer to his question about obedience do you think Brabantio expects from Desdemona?*

ANSWER. Brabantio seems to expect Desdemona to say that she owes obedience to her father above all.

LINE 187. *As director, how would you have Desdemona present herself in this speech? Should she appear very much as her father has described her, or should she be different?*

ANSWER. Desdemona's speech calls for a degree of self-assurance and assertiveness that would not have been predicted on the basis of her father's description. Apparently, Brabantio does not know his daughter well.

LINE 196. *What emotion does Brabantio seem to be expressing at the end of this speech?*

ANSWER. Brabantio appears to be expressing defeat or resignation to a situation he dislikes but knows he cannot change.

LINE 207. *How would you characterize the duke's speech to Brabantio? Can you think of other occasions when speeches like this one are delivered by persons in authority?*

ANSWER. The duke's speech is a series of platitudes or proverbs, offered as counsel and consolation to Brabantio in his time of trouble. Similarly platitudinous speeches may be given by members of the clergy or by politicians at the scene of a disaster.

LINE 218. *Is Brabantio comforted by the duke's speech? How would you describe his reaction?*

ANSWER. Brabantio is not comforted; rather, he is annoyed and suggests cynically that the duke might not be so cheerful if he were the one who had lost something he valued.

LINE 226. *Note that with the duke's speech, the language of the play moves from poetry to prose. Why might this shift occur here?*

ANSWER. The duke is now talking about the pragmatic matter of preparing for war and is in essence issuing Othello his military orders.

LINE 250. *When Desdemona speaks these lines, she is unwittingly responding to an issue raised earlier in the play. What is the issue, and who raised it?*

ANSWER. Desdemona is unknowingly responding to Brabantio's statement that she could never be attracted to a man of another race.

LINE 270. *Actors and directors have interpreted the character of Othello in a variety of ways. How would you have Othello deliver this speech to the duke and the senators?*

ANSWER. Those who interpret Othello as essentially a noble character would probably give this speech an air of generous sincerity. Those who see Othello as self-dramatizing, vain, or self-deceiving might give it a tinge of pomposity or self-satisfaction.

*Drama Study Guide: **The Tragedy of Othello, the Moor of Venice***

LINE 286. *What double layers of meaning are present here? Which word would you emphasize in speaking the line?*

ANSWER. *Fair* and *black* are being used to indicate both color or complexion and moral values, with *fair* connoting good and *black,* evil. The duke, therefore, is saying that Othello, though dark in complexion, is fair in his moral values. *Black* is the most important word in the line.

LINE 289. *What recurring theme does Brabantio's warning to Othello highlight? As the play proceeds, notice how this speech can be seen as foreshadowing.*

ANSWER. Brabantio's warning echoes the theme of deceit versus honesty or loyalty versus betrayal that recurs throughout the play.

LINE 290. *Would you have Othello deliver this line as if he has full confidence in Desdemona's loyalty or as if he is already worried? What is the irony in the line?*

ANSWER. Most students will likely interpret the line as a sincere but ironic statement of faith in Desdemona. The irony is in Othello's belief in Iago's loyalty, which the audience already knows is misplaced, and in the fact that Othello will lose his life over the matter of Desdemona's fidelity, although it will be he, not she, who loses faith.

LINE 304. *How would you have Roderigo say this line?*

ANSWER. Most actors play Roderigo as a silly, shallow, self-dramatizing young man full of self-pity.

LINE 312. *For what purpose does Iago use animal imagery in this speech? How would you describe his tone?*

ANSWER. Iago uses animal imagery to belittle human beings. His tone is world-weary and cynical, with an air of superiority or condescension.

LINE 328. *What point about human destiny is Iago making in this long speech comparing human bodies to gardens?*

ANSWER. Iago is asserting that human beings can shape their fates if they use reason or will to control their instincts, including the instinct to love, which he equates with lust.

LINE 347. *Why does Iago keep telling Roderigo to put money in his purse?*

ANSWER. Iago is trying to get Roderigo to act like a practical man rather than a romantic or lust-driven fool. He also wants Roderigo to enrich himself so that he can be a ready source of cash for Iago.

LINE 374, STAGE DIRECTION. *Who leaves the stage here, and what does this make possible?*

ANSWER. Roderigo leaves. Iago, left alone onstage, can deliver a soliloquy, which reveals some of his thoughts to the audience.

LINE 378. *What does Iago's use of the word* sport *suggest about his motivation for plotting against Othello?*

ANSWER. Iago's use of *sport* suggests that he enjoys making others suffer even if he has nothing to gain from their destruction.

LINE 382. *According to these lines, what additional motive does Iago have for plotting against Othello?*

ANSWER. Iago is concerned that people may believe rumors that Othello has slept with Iago's wife.

LINE 386. *What do expressions like "How? How? Let's see" reveal about Iago's strategies and thought processes?*

ANSWER. They reveal that Iago is making up his plan to destroy Othello as he goes along, taking advantage of events as they occur and making use of his knowledge of Othello's character.

LINE 396. *What recurring imagery do the last two lines of Iago's soliloquy contain?*

ANSWER. The lines contain imagery of light and dark, of hell, and of monstrous or unnatural events.

Act II   Scene 1

BEFORE LINE 1, STAGE DIRECTION. *The scene has shifted from Venice to a seaport in Cyprus. What props or scenery would you use to show the change in setting?*

ANSWER. Scenery might include a painted backdrop or lighted scrim representing the sea and a simple wooden or stonelike structure representing a dock or a sea wall.

Drama Study Guide: ***The Tragedy of Othello, the Moor of Venice***

LINE 17. *If you were staging the play, would you attempt to show the storm at sea as described in these lines?*

ANSWER. Shakespeare's description of the storm is so evocative that showing the actual scene is unnecessary. A storm scene would probably be more effective in a filmed, rather than a staged, version of the play.

LINE 51. *What first impression of Cassio does this speech give the audience?*

ANSWER. Cassio comes across as a gentleman of extravagant gesture and speech who is sincerely concerned about the welfare of his general.

AFTER LINE 51, STAGE DIRECTION. *In many of the theaters of Shakespeare's day, the main playing area was in the open air, whereas the offstage area was enclosed. That is why this stage direction calls for a cry from "within." Why might Shakespeare want the cry to come from offstage?*

ANSWER. A cry from offstage allows a director to avoid mounting a crowd scene, which would require a large number of appropriately costumed actors.

LINES 53–54. *What is the theatrical purpose of these two lines?*

ANSWER. These lines explain the meaning of the offstage cries and eliminate the need for a crowd scene.

LINES 56–57. *The stage direction calls for the sound of guns firing. These two lines explain its meaning. Why is the explanation necessary in this case?*

ANSWER. The explanation tells the audience that the gunfire is a salute to friendly ships rather than shots fired at an approaching enemy.

LINE 74. *Here Cassio continues his extravagant praise of Desdemona. How would you have him deliver these lines?*

ANSWER. Most directors and actors present Cassio as a young romantic in love with the sound of his own voice who nevertheless truly respects Othello and Desdemona. A few productions have suggested that Cassio is in love with Desdemona, but true to the code of the officer and the gentleman, he behaves honorably.

LINE 82, STAGE DIRECTION. *How would you have Desdemona and the others look as they meet the party on the shore?*

ANSWER. The travelers should appear tired and disheveled after their rough sail on a stormy sea.

LINE 88. *How do you interpret Desdemona's crisp reply to Cassio's high-flown welcoming speech?*

ANSWER. While remaining courteous, Desdemona is thinking very little about Cassio and a great deal about Othello.

AFTER LINE 99, STAGE DIRECTION. *How would you have Cassio kiss Emilia? What would you have this gesture reveal about his character?*

ANSWER. Cassio might kiss Emilia boldly, revealing that he is less respectful toward women of a lower social class than toward those of a higher class. Or he might kiss her with a confident swagger, in a way that is not disrespectful but rather reveals that he fancies himself irresistible to women of all classes.

LINE 111. *In contrast to Cassio's speeches, what does this speech reveal about Iago's attitude toward women?*

ANSWER. Unlike the smooth-talking, idealizing Cassio, Iago is blunt, unromantic, cynical, and suspicious when it comes to women.

LINE 112. *In your opinion, how might Desdemona take Iago's remarks about women?*

ANSWER. Desdemona is probably amused by the cleverness of Iago's remarks and not bothered by their cynicism.

LINE 118. *Knowledge of oneself and of others is a recurring motif in the play. What does this remark reveal about Iago's knowledge of himself?*

ANSWER. The line reveals that Iago knows himself well even though he rarely presents himself as he truly is.

LINE 122. *What recurring theme does Desdemona echo here? As the play proceeds, consider how well Desdemona really knows herself and others.*

ANSWER. Desdemona's lines recall the theme of appearance versus reality or the difficulty of knowing another person's true nature.

LINE 135. *What contrasting imagery that recurs throughout the play does Iago take up in his extended wordplay on the subject of women?*

ANSWER. Iago makes use of the contrasting images of light and dark and fair and black, playing on both their literal and their figurative meanings.

LINE 159. *What emotion would you have Desdemona express in response to Iago's final characterization of women?*

*Drama Study Guide: **The Tragedy of Othello, the Moor of Venice***

HRW MATERIAL COPYRIGHTED UNDER NOTICE APPEARING EARLIER IN THIS WORK.

39

ANSWER. *Most students will agree that by this point, Desdemona is more appalled than amused by Iago's mean-spirited attack.*

? LINE 175. *Unlike a soliloquy, an aside is spoken by a character who is not alone onstage but turns away from the other characters and addresses the audience. Besides the stage direction in brackets, what in this speech indicates that it is to be spoken as an aside?*

ANSWER. In line 166, Iago instructs himself to "whisper."

? LINE 175. *Although there is no stage direction calling for such an action, what does Iago's speech clearly indicate that Cassio has done?*

ANSWER. Iago's speech indicates that Cassio has smiled, put his fingers to his lips, and presumably kissed Desdemona's hand.

? LINE 189. *With what tone of voice and gestures would you have Othello deliver these lines?*

ANSWER. Most students will agree that Othello should speak with rapture and excitement. His pleasure is so keen that it approaches pain, or at least anxiety (he might clutch his heart), when he speaks of dying at the height of his happiness.

? LINE 197. *What emotion or emotions would you have Iago reveal in this aside?*

ANSWER. Iago's words suggest envy, hatred, and a desire for revenge.

? LINE 203. *How would you have Othello deliver these remarks about prattling and doting?*

ANSWER. Many students will see Othello as unused to the language of love and somewhat embarrassed by the new, tender emotions he is feeling and trying to express.

? LINE 245. *What is Iago trying to convince Roderigo of in this long speech? What arguments does he offer to support his claim?*

ANSWER. Iago wants Roderigo to believe that Desdemona has grown tired of Othello and is now attracted to Cassio. He argues that Othello is old and unattractive whereas Cassio is young and handsome and an opportunist who will take full advantage of Desdemona's waning interest in Othello.

? LINE 251. *What palpable proof of Desdemona and Cassio's involvement does Iago offer Roderigo?*

ANSWER. Iago reminds Roderigo that Cassio kissed Desdemona's hand.

? LINE 253. *Is Roderigo convinced by this "proof"?*

ANSWER. Roderigo remains unconvinced.

? LINE 261. *How does Iago finally get Roderigo to do as he wishes?*

ANSWER. By expounding on Cassio's lust, Iago begins to affect Roderigo by stirring up his lust for Desdemona. Finally, though, Iago simply issues orders to the weak-willed Roderigo, overpowering him with the force of his own will.

? LINE 273. *How does Iago use his knowledge of Cassio's character to plot against him? As the play proceeds, look for other instances where Iago uses his knowledge of others to do them harm.*

ANSWER. Knowing that Cassio has a hot temper, Iago plots to have Roderigo provoke Cassio's anger and thereby cause a disturbance that will put Cassio in a bad position with Othello.

? LINE 287. *In this soliloquy, how does what Iago says about Desdemona and Othello differ from what he has said about them to Roderigo? How do you explain the differences?*

ANSWER. In his soliloquy, Iago says that he does not believe that Desdemona loves Cassio (as he insisted to Roderigo), although he thinks he can convince others that she does. He admits that Othello is a loving husband who probably makes Desdemona happy and that he is not an old bore of whom she has already grown tired, as he suggested to Roderigo. Iago manipulates the truth when speaking to Roderigo in order to get Roderigo to do what he wants.

? LINE 308. *What attitude about his schemes would you have Iago display in this scene-ending soliloquy?*

ANSWER. Iago might display vengeful glee at the thought of destroying the two men he hates and envies. He might also display pride and satisfaction in the cleverness of his plots. Or he might be so cold and calculating that he displays little emotion.

Scene 3

? BEFORE LINE 1, STAGE DIRECTION. *The scene has shifted from outdoors to indoors. What might this suggest about the action to come?*

ANSWER. This shift might suggest a greater

*Drama Study Guide: **The Tragedy of Othello, the Moor of Venice***

emphasis on domestic or private concerns and less emphasis on public matters.

? LINE 3. *What does Othello warn Cassio against in this speech?*

ANSWER. Othello warns Cassio against losing self-control during the evening's celebration, when discipline will be relaxed.

? LINE 6. *What is the effect of the repeated use of the word* honest *in connection with Iago?*

ANSWER. The repetition emphasizes the irony that Iago is exactly the opposite of what he appears to be and that his deceptiveness, rather than his honesty, is complete: He has fooled everyone.

? LINE 10. *In this speech to Desdemona, how would Othello's tone differ from that in his exchange with Cassio?*

ANSWER. Here Othello is likely speaking in the tones of an eager lover, whereas in the exchange with Cassio he would have used the prudent tone of a military commander addressing a subordinate about his professional duty.

? LINE 43. *In what two ways does Iago try to tempt Cassio in this scene? Does he succeed?*

ANSWER. First Iago tries to draw Cassio into lecherous talk about Desdemona. Then he tries to induce Cassio (against his better judgment) to drink with the local gentlemen. In the first case, Cassio remains respectful in his responses; in the second case he gives in.

? LINE 57. *Once again Iago, left alone on the stage, reveals the devious way in which his mind works. Would you have him address the audience directly or appear as if he is thinking out loud, addressing himself only?*

ANSWER. Some students may want Iago to address the members of the audience directly to increase his intimacy with them. Others may want to create a clinical effect, as if the members of the audience were observing Iago's mind at work without his knowledge.

? AFTER LINE 63, STAGE DIRECTION. *What role is Iago playing here? How would you have him perform this drinking song?*

ANSWER. Most students will agree that Iago is playing the role of the merrymaking soldier. Some may say that he should play the role convincingly, whereas others may have him play it awkwardly. Perhaps Iago, the consummate actor, can play any part well; perhaps the part of a fun-loving carouser is beyond his range.

? LINE 74. *Why, in your opinion, did Shakespeare include this material on the relative drinking capacities of various European groups?*

ANSWER. Shakespeare probably included this low comic material to amuse his English audience and provide some relief from the tragic story of Othello's destruction.

? LINE 110. *How would you have Cassio deliver this speech?*

ANSWER. Cassio is drunk and is trying to convince himself and others that he is not. He might slur his speech and move as if having difficulty maintaining his balance.

? LINE 129. *What does Montano now believe about Cassio as a result of Iago's manipulations?*

ANSWER. Montano believes that Cassio is an inveterate drunkard who is not worthy of Othello's trust.

? LINE 138, STAGE DIRECTION. *Whose voice is crying "Help!" offstage?*

ANSWER. Roderigo is crying for help.

? LINE 144. *Would you play the fight scene between Roderigo and Cassio straight or with a touch of comedy?*

ANSWER. Some students may choose to play the scene seriously. Others may play it as slapstick, with Roderigo as the comic coward and Cassio as the loud, drunken soldier looking for a fight.

? LINE 157. *Iago is again pretending to be what he is not. What is he pretending? What role does he play here?*

ANSWER. Iago is pretending not to know who rang the alarm bell (it was he who told Roderigo to "cry a mutiny!"). He is playing the role of peacemaker and concerned protector of Cassio's reputation.

? LINE 157, STAGE DIRECTION. *How would you have Othello make his entrance?*

ANSWER. Othello might enter hurriedly, in a state of irritation and anxiety after being roused from his pleasant sleep beside Desdemona.

? LINE 172. *In what tone of voice would you have Othello speak to Cassio and Montano? How might his tone change when he speaks to Iago in the last two lines?*

ANSWER. Othello speaks to Montano and Cassio with anger. When he speaks to Iago, his tone is most likely warm and confident.

LINE 183. *Why, in your opinion, does Cassio decline to respond to Othello?*

ANSWER. Some students may say that Cassio is too ashamed to speak. Others may say he has become disoriented by the alcohol and the excitement and needs time to recover his composure.

LINE 211. *What is Othello's emotional state as he delivers this speech? What has brought him to this state?*

ANSWER. Othello is barely controlling a violent rage at Cassio and Montano, who have failed to give him a satisfactory explanation for fighting while they are supposed to be keeping the peace "in a town of war / Yet wild, the people's hearts brimful of fear."

LINE 216. *How would you have Iago deliver these blatantly hypocritical words?*

ANSWER. Iago, whose purpose is to deceive Othello, should deliver these lines with convincing sincerity.

LINE 243. *What flaws in Othello's character are revealed in this speech?*

ANSWER. Othello reveals that he is unable to distinguish between appearance and reality and is prone to making hasty, blind judgments about those closest to him.

LINE 245. *To whom is Othello speaking?*

ANSWER. Othello is addressing Cassio.

LINE 259. *What is Cassio likely feeling as he speaks about his lost reputation?*

ANSWER. Cassio likely feels great sorrow, regret, and shame because, through his own actions, he has lost something he values highly.

LINE 270. *What tone does Iago assume in response to Cassio's dejection?*

ANSWER. Iago plays the role of the resourceful, practical man of the world who sees reputations as based only on appearances and therefore open to

manipulation. He also presents himself as Cassio's helpful and concerned friend.

LINE 277. *What imagery does Cassio use to describe the effects of drinking? What larger themes in the play do these images reflect?*

ANSWER. Cassio uses images of animals, hell, and the devil. The animal imagery reflects the theme of civilization versus barbarism that runs through the play. The diabolical imagery reflects the tension between the heavenly and the infernal impulses that are at war for the soul of Othello and are personified by Desdemona and Iago respectively.

LINE 315. *How does Iago characterize Desdemona when advising Cassio to seek her help? As the play proceeds, decide whether this description is accurate.*

ANSWER. Iago describes Desdemona as so generous and willing to help others that she generally does even more than she is asked.

LINE 353. *Notice the imagery of disease, hunting, and trapping that Iago uses to describe his plotting. What attitude toward his own machinations would you have Iago project in this soliloquy?*

ANSWER. Most students will agree that Iago takes pride and pleasure in his ability to manipulate and harm others. He is cold, calculating, and without conscience.

LINE 360. *How would you have Roderigo deliver this speech to Iago? Consider his tone of voice and posture.*

ANSWER. Roderigo would most likely deliver this speech in a whining, self-pitying tone of voice, perhaps cringing slightly, like a beaten dog.

LINE 379. *What is the effect of having Iago reveal his plans to the audience?*

ANSWER. Most students will say that knowing what Iago plans increases the audience's sense of dread and apprehension. It also gives the audience the opportunity to enjoy the spectacle of Iago's clever villainy, and all audiences love a good villain.

Act III   Scene 1

LINE 1. *Why might Cassio ask the musicians to play in front of the castle where Othello and Desdemona are staying?*

ANSWER. Perhaps Cassio wishes to make amends to Othello or put him in a forgiving mood.

LINE 20. *This scene between the clown and the musician, which provides low comic relief, is often dropped by directors who wish to create a uniformly tragic mood in the play. Would you keep the scene or drop it? Why?*

ANSWER. Some students may see the scene as adding nothing and detracting from the play's emotional intensity and quick movement forward. Others may not want the audience to miss Shakespeare's amusing wordplay and clever put-down humor.

LINE 26. *How is the clown used to further the action of the main plot?*

ANSWER. Cassio pays the clown to ask Emilia to come and speak with him.

LINE 37. *What is the effect of having Cassio speak of Iago in language very similar to Othello's?*

ANSWER. The similarity in the words used by Cassio and Othello underscores the fact that both men are taken in by Iago, and both tend to be deceived by appearances.

LINE 47. *What is Emilia's attitude toward Cassio?*

ANSWER. Emilia is sympathetic to Cassio and wants to help him. She also reassures him that Othello is already softening toward him.

Scene 2

BEFORE LINE 1, STAGE DIRECTION. *After you read this short scene, decide what type of room you think these events would take place in.*

ANSWER. Since Othello is conducting state business, the scene should probably take place in a library or some other formal and imposing room.

Scene 3

BEFORE LINE 1, STAGE DIRECTION. *This long scene takes place in the garden of the castle. What events are traditionally associated with gardens?*

ANSWER. Gardens, especially the garden of Eden, are associated with fertility, love, innocence, and temptation.

LINE 5. *Who besides Othello and Cassio is taken in by Iago?*

ANSWER. Desdemona and Emilia also believe in Iago's honesty and good intentions.

LINE 28. *Why, in your opinion, is Desdemona determined to help Cassio?*

ANSWER. Some students may think that Desdemona is simply sympathetic and generous by nature. Others may think she is testing the strength of her influence on Othello. A few may see her as nagging and meddlesome, needlessly risking the happiness of her new marriage.

LINE 50. *What is the irony in this statement by Desdemona?*

ANSWER. The irony, which the audience can appreciate but Desdemona cannot, is that where Iago is concerned, she cannot judge honesty by the look on the face.

LINE 83. *What is the immediate effect of Desdemona's persistent pleading for Cassio? What might be an effect in the long term?*

ANSWER. The immediate effect is that a weary Othello gives in to Desdemona's wishes. In the long term she may arouse Othello's suspicion of the reason for her insistence.

LINE 89. *What do you think of Desdemona's knowledge of herself and her situation? Is she as obedient as she sees herself, for example?*

ANSWER. Students may recognize that Desdemona is not always accurate in her knowledge of herself. She ultimately does obey her husband and leave him alone, but for a long while before that she presses on when he clearly wants her to stop.

LINE 92. *What emotion is Othello expressing in this speech?*

ANSWER. Othello is expressing a kind of desperate love and anxiety as he realizes that his happiness depends on his love for Desdemona.

LINE 105. *What strategy is Iago using to stir up Othello?*

ANSWER. Iago is being cryptic and insinuating, dropping hints and acting as if he knew more than he is telling.

LINE 133. *How does Othello react to Iago's strategy?*

ANSWER. Othello is growing irritated and apprehensive. He strongly suspects that Iago is withholding some disturbing information.

LINE 161. *What speech earlier in the play does this one echo? How does the tone of Iago's remarks differ from that of the previous speech?*

ANSWER. This speech echoes Cassio's speech in

Act II, Scene 3, lines 256–259. Unlike Cassio, Iago speaks insincerely here, spouting platitudes that are in direct contrast to what he said earlier (Act II, Scene 3, lines 262–264).

? LINE 162. *How would you have Othello deliver this line?*

ANSWER. Othello should show impatience, irritation, and authority as he speaks this line.

? LINE 167. *What is the double irony in Iago's warning to Othello about the dangers of jealousy?*

ANSWER. The most obvious irony is that Iago is deliberately trying to work Othello into a state of jealousy while piously warning him against it. The second irony is that Iago himself is driven by jealousy and may himself fall victim to jealousy's destructive powers.

? LINE 192. *What do these lines about doubt and proof tell about Othello's temperament?*

ANSWER. They reveal that Othello does not have much tolerance for uncertainty; once suspicious, he wants his doubts resolved quickly one way or the other. He is man of action, not reflection.

? LINE 204. *How does Iago begin sowing doubts about Desdemona in these lines?*

ANSWER. Iago observes that Venetian women of Desdemona's class are known for deceiving their husbands and hiding their misdeeds.

? LINE 208. *What further argument against Desdemona's honesty does Iago make here?*

ANSWER. Iago points out that Desdemona fooled her father about her feelings toward Othello.

? LINE 213. *What do you think Othello means when he says he is "bound" to Iago forever? What unintended meanings might the line convey?*

ANSWER. Othello means that he is bound, or obligated, to Iago out of a sense of gratitude for his friendship and service. The line might also mean that the men are bound together by a common fate or a common flaw.

? LINE 225. *Do you think Othello means what he says about Desdemona? How would you have him deliver this line?*

ANSWER. Most students will agree that Othello is still hanging on to his faith in Desdemona, but his peace of mind has definitely been shaken by Iago's insinuations.

? LINE 238. *What view of Desdemona's actions does Iago insinuate into this speech?*

ANSWER. Iago suggests that it was unnatural for Desdemona to reject suitors of her own background in favor of Othello and that it is reasonable to expect that she will come to regret her decision.

? LINE 243. *What emotions does Othello express in these lines?*

ANSWER. Othello expresses anxiety, suspicion, and perhaps self-pity.

? LINE 265. *What insecurities does Othello express here that seem to fuel his suspicion of Desdemona?*

ANSWER. Othello worries about his dark complexion, his lack of courtly manners, and his declining youth.

? LINE 276. *In this speech, Othello begins to echo ideas and images used earlier by Iago. What types of imagery previously associated with Iago does Othello now use? Watch for similar appropriations of Iago's language by Othello as the play proceeds.*

ANSWER. Othello appropriates Iago's imagery of animals ("toad"), torture ("dungeon"), and disease ("plague").

? LINE 278. *Suddenly Othello reverses himself and expresses restored faith in Desdemona. What may have caused this change?*

ANSWER. The appearance of Desdemona may have temporarily quieted Othello's fears. (She has just reentered with Emilia.)

? AFTER LINE 286, STAGE DIRECTION. *How would you have Othello push "the handkerchief from him"?*

ANSWER. Most students will suggest that Othello should push the handkerchief away with impatience, irritation, or indifference.

? LINE 307. *Why does Emilia take Desdemona's handkerchief and tell her husband that she has it?*

ANSWER. Emilia wishes to please Iago.

? LINE 317. *How does Iago respond to Emilia's telling him that she has Desdemona's handkerchief?*

ANSWER. He snatches it from her; he is ungrateful, surly, and secretive about his reasons for wanting it.

Drama Study Guide: ***The Tragedy of Othello, the Moor of Venice***

LINE 321. *What trifle "light as air" will Iago use to prove to Othello that his suspicions are valid?*

ANSWER. Iago will use Desdemona's handkerchief to prove to Othello that Desdemona has been unfaithful to him.

LINE 340. *How would you have Othello deliver these lines, in which he says that he wishes he were a husband who knew nothing of his wife's infidelities?*

ANSWER. Many students will find a false, self-pitying, and self-dramatizing note in this speech. If this tone is emphasized, the audience's sympathy for Othello as Iago's victim may be lessened.

LINE 354. *What do you think motivates Othello to give this farewell speech to his military career? What emotion would you want this speech to create in the audience?*

ANSWER. Othello seems to sense that since he has made Desdemona all-important and now suspects that she has betrayed him, his life will never be the same again. Students may want the audience to be saddened by the sight of Othello trapped in Iago's web or disappointed that Othello cannot see himself and others more clearly.

LINE 370. *What tone does Othello take with Iago in this and in the two preceding speeches?*

ANSWER. Othello is threatening and angry as he demands that Iago give him visible proof of Desdemona's infidelity.

LINE 380. *How does Iago respond to Othello?*

ANSWER. Iago plays the wronged friend who was only trying to help and is now being made to suffer for telling the truth.

LINE 387. *What state of mind is Othello expressing in this speech? What physical movements might an actor use to portray his state?*

ANSWER. Othello is betraying a state of unbearable doubt or uncertainty; he can't decide whom or what to believe. An actor playing Othello might hold his head as if it were about to burst with inner tension or look into a mirror searchingly when he speaks of his "begrimed and black" face.

LINE 423. *Othello asks Iago for proofs and reasons that will satisfy him that Desdemona has been disloyal. What does Iago offer Othello in this speech?*

ANSWER. Iago tells Othello that he heard Cassio,

while dreaming, profess his love for Desdemona and his hatred for Othello.

LINE 428. *How does this tone contrast with Othello's tone in the first two acts of the play?*

ANSWER. Othello's speech is becoming more violent and more savage and is full of references to animals and animal-like behavior.

LINE 457, STAGE DIRECTION. *For what purpose does Othello kneel here?*

ANSWER. He kneels to swear an oath of revenge against Cassio and Desdemona.

AFTER LINE 459, STAGE DIRECTION. *Why does Iago kneel?*

ANSWER. Iago kneels to pledge his service to Othello in seeking vengeance on Cassio and Desdemona.

LINE 475. *In this scene, Iago, like the serpent in the garden of Eden, has tempted Othello. What in this speech reveals a turning point in Othello's internal and external conflicts?*

ANSWER. Othello has now resolved his conflicts by accepting Iago's charges as true and deciding to kill Desdemona himself.

LINE 476. *What line earlier in the scene does this line echo?*

ANSWER. This line echoes line 213, in which Othello states that he is bound to Iago forever.

Scene 4

LINE 13. *What wordplay is the clown employing in his dialogue with Desdemona? What major theme of the play does his wordplay reflect?*

ANSWER. The clown is playing on the two meanings of the word *lie*: "to tell an untruth" and "to recline" or "to rest." His punning reflects the play's theme of deceit and betrayal.

LINE 25. *Why do you think Emilia lies to Desdemona about the handkerchief?*

ANSWER. Emilia lies to protect herself and Iago.

LINE 32. *In what way is Desdemona lying in these lines?*

ANSWER. She is consciously or unconsciously deceiving herself about Othello's capacity for jealousy.

*Drama Study Guide: **The Tragedy of Othello, the Moor of Venice***

HRW MATERIAL COPYRIGHTED UNDER NOTICE APPEARING EARLIER IN THIS WORK.

45

LINE 44. *What do these lines reveal about Othello's purpose in this meeting with Desdemona?*

ANSWER. Othello intends to deceive her by pretending he trusts her as before. His true purpose is to trap her into revealing her guilt. He is now behaving more like Iago and less like his former self.

LINE 84. *What is the effect on Desdemona of Othello's speeches about the handkerchief he gave her?*

ANSWER. Othello has given the handkerchief so much importance that Desdemona feels terrified and guilty about having mislaid it.

LINE 86. *Desdemona tells Othello twice that the handkerchief is not lost. In what tone of voice would you have her tell these two lies?*

ANSWER. Desdemona might first tell the lie tentatively, in a shaky voice, and then repeat it with more emphasis after Othello questions her further.

LINE 96. *What ploy is Desdemona attempting in order to draw Othello's attention from the handkerchief? How would you want the audience to respond to her efforts?*

ANSWER. Desdemona has resumed her pleas for Cassio's reinstatement, thinking this will distract Othello from the question of the missing handkerchief. Most students will want the audience to feel sympathy for the innocent Desdemona, who is no match for dissemblers like Iago and now Othello himself.

LINE 99. *What effect does Desdemona's behavior have on Othello in this scene?*

ANSWER. Othello is more convinced than ever of Desdemona's guilt. He has confirmed in his own mind the legitimacy of his feelings of anger and jealousy.

LINE 107. *How does Emilia's view of men differ from Desdemona's view of Othello?*

ANSWER. Emilia, older and more experienced, is realistic, even cynical, whereas Desdemona, young and inexperienced, is idealistic and perhaps ignorant of her husband's true nature.

LINE 126. *What is the irony in Desdemona's statement? What larger theme does it echo?*

ANSWER. Desdemona believes that Othello is not himself because of a passing mood or worry, but the audience knows that he has changed profoundly. Her statement recalls the theme of distinguishing appearance from reality, especially in judging others.

LINE 162. *What earlier speech do Emilia's comments on jealousy recall? How does her description of a jealous person fit Othello?*

ANSWER. Emilia's comparing jealousy to a monster that creates itself recalls Iago's "green-eyed monster" metaphor in Act III, Scene 3. Othello's jealousy does seem to increase without much substance to sustain it.

LINE 171. *How would you have Cassio deliver these lines to Bianca?*

ANSWER. Most students will agree that Cassio should deliver these lines lovingly, showing a desire to placate Bianca.

LINE 176. *How would you have Bianca deliver these lines to Cassio?*

ANSWER. Most students will agree that Bianca should speak like a woman who misses her beloved and wonders why she has not seen him for a week.

LINE 183. *How does Bianca behave here? What other characters have behaved similarly?*

ANSWER. She is jealous and suspicious because Cassio has given her a handkerchief that she believes belongs to another woman. Her behavior recalls the jealousy of both Othello and Roderigo.

LINE 188. *Is Cassio telling the truth? How did the handkerchief get into his chamber?*

ANSWER. Cassio is telling the truth. Iago secretly put the handkerchief in Cassio's room.

LINE 200. *How would you have Cassio take leave of Bianca here?*

ANSWER. Some students will say that Cassio is in good humor and eager to pacify Bianca. Others will see him as impatient with Bianca, and undoubtedly far less interested in her than in his standing with Othello.

Act IV   Scene 1

LINE 22. *What images that Othello uses here were associated with Iago earlier in the play? What does this appropriation of Iago's images suggest?*

ANSWER. Othello uses imagery of an animal (a bird) and disease. This appropriation suggests that he has aligned himself with Iago or become more like his ancient.

LINE 37. *How are the two meanings of the word* lie *being used here?*

ANSWER. Iago is suggesting that Cassio would *lie* or tell an untruth about *lying,* or sleeping, with Desdemona.

AFTER LINE 44, STAGE DIRECTION. *Although the direction calls for Othello to fall into a "trance," the subsequent text makes it clear that Othello is having an epileptic seizure. Many directors have chosen to cut this scene or alter it significantly. How would you handle the need to get Othello out of the way for a little while so that Iago can set up the scene with Cassio?*

ANSWER. Some students might simply have Othello faint, without showing the dramatic symptoms of an epileptic episode. In that case, the text would have to be altered slightly.

LINE 46. *What does the image Iago uses here reveal about how he sees himself?*

ANSWER. That Iago sees himself as a doctor administering medicine reveals his concern with having control over the lives of others.

LINE 65. *In this dialogue between Iago and Othello, there are a number of references to men, beasts, and monsters. How does this language reflect what is going on within Othello?*

ANSWER. Othello is progressively losing his rationality and thus his humanity and is acting more and more like a madman, a monster, or a beast.

LINE 66. *Several times in this scene, Iago urges Othello to behave like "a man." What is ironic about this admonition?*

ANSWER. It is ironic that after doing everything he can to madden Othello with jealousy and suspicion, Iago chides him for not acting rationally, that is, like "a man."

LINE 88. *What does Iago want Othello to do while Iago is speaking to Cassio?*

ANSWER. Iago wants Othello to stand at a distance from him and Cassio so that he can observe Cassio's demeanor when Iago supposedly draws him out on the subject of his relationship with Desdemona.

AFTER LINE 93, STAGE DIRECTION. *In your production, where onstage would you place Othello?*

ANSWER. Othello might peer around a wall or a column or stand on a balcony or at a window above Cassio and Iago.

LINE 100. *Again Iago reveals his strategy to the audience in a soliloquy. What is his plan?*

ANSWER. Iago plans to tease Cassio about Bianca so that he will talk and gesture gaily and Othello, observing from a distance, will assume that he is joking about his relationship with Desdemona.

AFTER LINE 107, STAGE DIRECTION. *Why must Iago speak in a softer voice?*

ANSWER. Iago must be sure that Othello does not hear him speaking of Bianca rather than Desdemona.

LINE 115. *What do the speeches that come between Iago and Cassio's dialogue show that Othello is doing? What does Othello's behavior show about his state of mind?*

ANSWER. The speeches show that Othello is interpreting Cassio's movements in light of what Iago has told him and what he already believes about Cassio and Desdemona. This behavior shows how irrational Othello has become.

LINE 135. *How would you direct the actor playing Cassio to deliver this speech and his next one?*

ANSWER. Most students will see the need to have the actor use his body actively, miming Bianca's clinging to him, so that Othello will have a lot of material on which to project his fears and his fantasies.

LINE 154. *How would you have Bianca deliver this speech to Cassio?*

ANSWER. Most students will agree that Bianca should show anger, indignation, and jealousy.

LINE 183. *How does this prose speech of Othello's reflect his state of mind?*

ANSWER. This speech embodies Othello's conflicting emotions and irrational state of mind as he is racked simultaneously by hate and love for Desdemona.

? **LINE 189.** *What attitude toward Desdemona is Iago now taking? How does it differ from his prior stance?*

ANSWER. Iago is now criticizing Desdemona whenever Othello praises her, reminding him of her supposed iniquity. In the previous act, Iago pretended to favor mercy for her and revenge only on Cassio.

? **LINE 206.** *With what emotion would you have Othello speak about the justice of killing Desdemona in her bed, as Iago has just suggested?*

ANSWER. Some students will say that Othello should speak with the stern voice of a righteous judge. Others will say that he feels a desire for revenge, not the need for justice.

? **LINE 229.** *Note the proliferation of images of hell in Othello's speeches as this scene continues. What do you think causes this particular outburst?*

ANSWER. Most students will agree that Othello is reacting to Desdemona's reference in the preceding line to her "love" for Cassio.

? **LINE 235.** *Some actors playing Othello, such as the great nineteenth-century American Edwin Booth, refused to hit Desdemona, believing that this action detracted too much from the essential nobility of Othello's character. Would you include the slap in your production?*

ANSWER. Many students will say that the slap should be included, to serve as a precursor to the greater violence to come.

? **LINE 242.** *What do you think Desdemona is feeling as she delivers this line?*

ANSWER. Desdemona is probably feeling fear, pain, confusion, shock, and perhaps some indignation.

? **LINE 249.** *What play on words is Othello making in this line?*

ANSWER. Othello is playing on the literal and figurative meanings of *turn*. He is saying that Desdemona can change the direction in which she moves her body and she can change the object of her affections and her loyalty.

? **LINE 264.** *How would you answer Lodovico's question? Do you think Othello is insane?*

ANSWER. Most students will agree that although Othello has been greatly manipulated by Iago, he had the wits to evaluate Iago's suggestions and is therefore responsible for his actions.

Scene 2

? **LINE 11.** *In the course of this interrogation of Emilia by Othello, what is Othello's attitude toward Emilia and Desdemona?*

ANSWER. Othello has already made up his mind that Desdemona is guilty, and he is not disposed to believe anything Emilia says to him.

? **LINE 16.** *This is the first of several ironic statements in which Emilia curses the person who has slandered Desdemona. What is the irony?*

ANSWER. The irony is that Emilia does not realize what the audience knows: that her husband, Iago, is the person who has slandered Desdemona. This is an instance of dramatic irony.

? **LINE 23.** *How would you describe this speech of Othello's? What does it reveal about his character at this point in the play?*

ANSWER. Othello's speech is coarse, suspicious, and vindictive. It is that of a character obsessed with mad or criminal thoughts.

? **LINE 30.** *In what terms is Othello addressing Emilia here?*

ANSWER. Othello is addressing Emilia as if she were the keeper of a brothel, a house of prostitution.

? **LINE 32.** *How would you have Desdemona deliver these lines?*

ANSWER. Most students will agree that Desdemona should express fear and perplexity.

? **LINE 37.** *What is Othello's purpose in having Desdemona swear that she is honest? Would you have Othello seize hold of Desdemona during this speech?*

ANSWER. Othello wants Desdemona to be damned for swearing falsely as well as for being unfaithful. Some directors have had Othello seize Desdemona and force her to her knees.

? **LINE 40.** *How would you have Othello's tone change here?*

ANSWER. Othello's tone might change from vindictiveness and anger to disgust, sadness, or self-pity.

*Drama Study Guide: **The Tragedy of Othello, the Moor of Venice***

? LINE 46. *In this speech, what explanation does Desdemona come up with for Othello's strange behavior? How do you feel toward her at this point?*

ANSWER. Desdemona speculates that Othello is angry with her because he believes that her father is behind his recall to Venice. Most students will express a great deal of sympathy for Desdemona, who does not even understand what she is being accused of.

? LINE 63. *In what tone would you have Othello deliver this speech about his sufferings? How might an audience react to him?*

ANSWER. Formerly these lines were often played to elicit sympathy for Othello, who believes he has lost what he loves most. Most modern interpretations, however, stress Othello's self-pity and egocentric concern for his reputation. Students may note that audience members who are feeling a great deal of sympathy for Desdemona in this scene may have difficulty sympathizing with her accuser at the same time.

? LINE 85. *With what emotion would you have Desdemona say this line?*

ANSWER. Most directors have Desdemona protest her innocence here with an assertiveness or with a sense of injustice or injury that is greater now that she is beginning to understand what she is being accused of.

? LINE 89, STAGE DIRECTION. *The stage direction calls for Othello to raise his voice. What emotion do you think he is meant to be expressing?*

ANSWER. Most students will agree that Othello is meant to express mad rage or hysterical anger.

? LINE 113. *How would you describe Desdemona's mental state as she says these lines?*

ANSWER. Students may say that Desdemona is dazed, shocked, or depressed.

? LINE 119. *What is the effect of having Desdemona decline to say the word with which Othello has branded her and instead having Emilia supply the word?*

ANSWER. A contrast is created between Desdemona's shocked innocence and Emilia's knowledge of men and the world.

? LINE 147. *What is Iago's reaction to Emilia's giving voice to her suspicion that some malicious person has poisoned Othello's mind with false accusations against Desdemona?*

ANSWER. The accuracy of Emilia's suspicions makes Iago uneasy, and since he is the guilty party, he is trying to silence her.

? LINE 163. *In this speech, Desdemona affirms her love for Othello despite his unjust accusations. How would you want an audience to react to her devotion?*

ANSWER. Some students may want an audience to be moved and impressed by Desdemona's steadfast love and loyalty. Others may want the audience to disapprove of her willingness to accept Othello's injustice passively.

? LINE 188. *What is Roderigo's complaint against Iago in this scene?*

ANSWER. Roderigo is complaining because he has given a lot of money to Iago for Iago to use to gain Desdemona's affections, yet Roderigo is still waiting to enjoy her favors.

? LINE 215. *What strategies does Iago use to persuade Roderigo to work with him awhile longer?*

ANSWER. First Iago compliments Roderigo on his intelligence and courage. Then he appeals to Roderigo's impatient lust by promising that he will "enjoy" Desdemona the very next night.

? LINE 236. *How does Iago trick Roderigo into furthering Iago's own interests?*

ANSWER. Iago pretends that he wants Roderigo to kill Cassio in order to keep Othello and Desdemona in Cyprus.

? LINE 242. *Why do you think Shakespeare used all prose here?*

ANSWER. Shakespeare may have used prose to emphasize the pragmatic and seamy nature of this conversation.

Scene 3

? LINE 9. *In what tone of voice would you have Othello deliver this line?*

ANSWER. Most students will agree that Othello should speak harshly and imperiously, as if Desdemona were his servant.

? LINE 18. *How does Desdemona's attitude toward Othello's behavior differ from Emilia's?*

ANSWER. Desdemona bears Othello's ill humor patiently and without complaint, whereas Emilia angrily criticizes him.

LINE 25. *How do you interpret Desdemona's request that she be shrouded in her wedding sheets?*

ANSWER. Many students will see her request as a premonition of her early death. Others will see it as a sign of her melancholy mood. Some students may also note the irony as Desdemona cherishes a symbol of her marriage even as the marriage is leading to her undoing.

LINE 40. *What do the maid Barbary, the lady from Venice whom Emilia mentions here, and Desdemona all have in common?*

ANSWER. All three women are devoted to men who are keeping their distance for reasons that are not clear to them.

BEFORE LINE 41, STAGE DIRECTION. *In what tone of voice would you have Desdemona sing this song?*

ANSWER. Most students will agree that Desdemona should sing sadly and mournfully.

LINE 64. *What is Desdemona asking Emilia?*

ANSWER. Desdemona wants to know whether Emilia would ever cheat on her husband.

LINE 77. *Has Emilia answered Desdemona's question honestly? How would you characterize her reply?*

ANSWER. Most students will agree that Emilia has responded honestly. Her reply can be described as realistic, unromantic, and pragmatic.

LINE 83. *Desdemona expresses disbelief that any woman would betray her husband. Do you think a character of such innocence could be made credible to a modern audience?*

ANSWER. Some students will say that if Desdemona is played as very young and very sheltered, her romantic idealism may be made credible. Others may say that if she is played as an immature woman who refuses to look at life and her husband as they really are, her character will be credible.

LINE 103. *According to Emilia, why are some women unfaithful to their husbands?*

ANSWER. Emilia says that husbands, because they are stingy, jealous, and violent, give their wives ample reason to be unhappy. Furthermore, they often set a bad example by being unfaithful to their wives.

LINE 105. *What is Desdemona's response to Emilia's indictment of husbands' behavior?*

ANSWER. In essence, Desdemona says that two wrongs do not make a right, that a wife's infidelity cannot be justified by a husband's misdeeds.

Act V   Scene 1

BEFORE LINE 1, STAGE DIRECTION. *The setting has now moved to a street some distance from the castle. What kind of action do you expect in this scene? As you read the dialogue, look for clues to the presence or absence of light.*

ANSWER. Many students will expect violent action.

LINE 6. *With what body movements and tone of voice would you have Roderigo deliver this line?*

ANSWER. Many students will suggest that Roderigo hold his sword with trembling hands and speak in a quavering voice.

LINE 10. *What action would you have Roderigo make as he speaks these words?*

ANSWER. Roderigo undoubtedly draws his sword.

LINE 22. *Would you have Iago make this speech within earshot of Roderigo or as an aside to the audience?*

ANSWER. This speech must be made outside Roderigo's hearing because in it Iago confesses that he would be happy to have Roderigo as well as Cassio killed, since either one could expose his schemes.

AFTER LINE 22, STAGE DIRECTION. *What does this indicate Roderigo is to do?*

ANSWER. Roderigo is to thrust his sword at Cassio.

LINE 26. *What does Cassio's speech reveal about Roderigo's action?*

ANSWER. Cassio's words reveal that the thickness of his coat has protected him from Roderigo's sword. He is unharmed or merely grazed.

Drama Study Guide: The Tragedy of Othello, the Moor of Venice

LINE 36. *What is Othello's reaction when he thinks that Cassio has been wounded and is dying?*

ANSWER. Othello is grateful to Iago for attacking Cassio and is emboldened by Iago's violent example to go on with his plan to kill Desdemona in her bed.

LINE 44. *How do the Venetian gentlemen, Gratiano and Lodovico, respond to the cries that they hear coming from the wounded men? Why do they respond as they do?*

ANSWER. The two gentlemen are afraid to investigate the cries on their own. They are frightened by the darkness and their unfamiliarity with the Cyprus streets.

AFTER LINE 46, STAGE DIRECTION. *What is the ironic significance of Iago's bringing light?*

ANSWER. Murder and treachery have been committed under cover of darkness; Iago's light will not illuminate anything or protect anyone.

LINE 59. *Iago is always pretending to be other than what he is. What role is he playing here?*

ANSWER. Iago, Cassio's assailant, is pretending that he doesn't know who attacked Cassio and that he wishes to protect Cassio from further harm.

LINE 62. *With what familiar imagery does the dying Roderigo condemn Iago, his murderer?*

ANSWER. Roderigo uses images of an animal and damnation.

LINE 77. *How would you have Bianca deliver this line?*

ANSWER. Most students will agree that Bianca is truly surprised and alarmed by Cassio's condition.

LINE 84. *Why does Iago ask for a garter and a chair? What role is he playing?*

ANSWER. Iago wants the garter to use as a tourniquet to stop Cassio's bleeding and the chair to carry Cassio since he cannot walk. Iago is playing the role of the resourceful rescuer.

LINE 89. *Why are there so many references to light in this scene?*

ANSWER. The lack of light helped Iago wound Cassio without being identified and kill Roderigo without being discovered. Figuratively, the lack of light reflects the characters' lack of knowledge of Iago's true nature.

LINE 111. *What does Iago say to try to cast suspicion on Bianca? What recurring theme does this reflect?*

ANSWER. Iago tries to suggest that Bianca's paleness and her stare are evidence of her guilt. His accusation reflects the recurring theme of mistaking appearances for reality.

LINE 130. *How might the audience be affected by Iago's last two lines in this scene?*

ANSWER. Members of the audience are likely to sense an increase in the dramatic tension, or suspense, as they await the play's final scene.

Scene 2

BEFORE LINE 1, STAGE DIRECTION. *Why might Shakespeare have called for Desdemona to be asleep when Othello comes to kill her?*

ANSWER. Most students will agree that having Desdemona sleeping emphasizes her innocence and vulnerability.

LINE 15. *What images does Othello use to describe the sleeping Desdemona?*

ANSWER. Othello uses images that evoke contrasting colors (blood—red; snow and alabaster—white) and contrasting natural forces (light and dark, heat and cold, growth and decay).

AFTER LINE 15, STAGE DIRECTION. *How do members of the audience most likely feel when Othello kisses the sleeping Desdemona while talking of killing her?*

ANSWER. The members of the audience most likely feel pity for the main characters and terror as they anticipate the events that are about to unfold.

LINE 32. *How would you have Othello speak to Desdemona about her soul? Do you think he is softening in his resolve to kill her?*

ANSWER. Many students will suggest that Othello is feeling some last-minute sympathy for Desdemona and so should speak gently. Other students may point out that Othello talks of sparing Desdemona's soul but not her body, and that his speech should betray his rage and hatred.

LINE 38. *How would you have Desdemona deliver this line?*

ANSWER. Many students will say that Desdemona should speak simply and with the amazement of a child who does not understand the evil around her.

Drama Study Guide: **The Tragedy of Othello, the Moor of Venice**

LINE 66. *How does Othello's tone seem to change in the course of this speech? What do you think is the cause of the change?*

ANSWER. Othello's tone seems to grow colder and angrier. The cause of the change may be Desdemona's denial of an adulterous relationship with Cassio, or it may be the mere mention of Cassio's name.

LINE 72. *How does Othello reply to Desdemona's suggestion that Cassio be asked about the handkerchief?*

ANSWER. Othello says that Cassio cannot speak because Iago has taken it upon himself to silence him permanently.

LINE 83. *How would you have Desdemona use her body and her voice at this point?*

ANSWER. Some students may have Desdemona attempt to put her arms around Othello and tearfully plead for her life. Others may have her clasp her hands in a gesture of prayer.

BEFORE LINE 84, STAGE DIRECTION. *The murder of Desdemona has been handled in many ways over the centuries. Some nineteenth-century actors playing Othello, such as the Italian Tommaso Salvini, have displayed volcanic physical violence, whereas others have acted quietly and with great solemnity, as if enacting a ritual execution or a religious sacrifice. How would you stage the murder?*

ANSWER. Some students may prefer to have Othello smother Desdemona with a pillow (rather than choke her or stab her, as has been done in some productions) and to commit the act behind the bed curtains so that the audience sees and hears little.

LINE 101. *What effect do Emilia's cries have on Othello?*

ANSWER. Emilia's cries do not keep Othello from committing the murder (lines 85–88), but when he realizes that he will have to admit Emilia to the chamber, he seems to begin to awaken to the consequences of his action (lines 97–101).

LINE 104. *How has Shakespeare solved the problem of concealing Desdemona from Emilia?*

ANSWER. The text indicates that the bed is decorated with curtains, which Othello closes to conceal Desdemona.

LINE 111. *What is the irony in Othello's statement?*

ANSWER. The irony is that Othello himself has been driven mad, though not by the moon. (His madness was caused by Iago's lies and his own flawed character.)

LINE 117. *Desdemona's speaking after Othello presumes her dead may strike the audience as improbable or even comic. How might a director maintain the solemn mood?*

ANSWER. Some students may suggest that Othello's attack on Desdemona should be neither too violent nor too drawn out so that her remaining alive is believable. Others may suggest that the stage be set up in such a way that the audience can see Desdemona stir on the bed even before this moment but the distracted Othello cannot.

LINE 121. *What action would you have accompany Emilia's words?*

ANSWER. Most students will agree that Emilia should run toward the bed, fling open the curtains, and perhaps lift the dying Desdemona.

LINE 125. *How would you have Desdemona say her last lines? What effect on the audience would you want to produce?*

ANSWER. Most students will agree that Desdemona should speak her last lines in a forgiving and loving tone, without anger or fear. Students will most likely want the audience to feel sad. Some might want the production to evoke in the audience either a sense of admiration for Desdemona or the feeling that a good life has been senselessly ended.

LINE 130. *Why does Othello confess so quickly to the murder of Desdemona?*

ANSWER. Some students will say that Othello's sense of honor and his belief that he was justified in killing Desdemona lead him to make a quick confession. Others will say that he is motivated by a guilty conscience.

LINE 139. *What are some of the contrasting images used by Othello and Emilia in the preceding angry exchange?*

ANSWER. The images include "false as water" and "heavenly true"; "the more angel she" and "thou art a devil"; and "water" and "fire."

LINE 152. *Why does Emilia repeat the word husband?*

ANSWER. Emilia repeats the word because she is having trouble believing what she is hearing—that Iago told the lies that led Othello to kill Desdemona.

*Drama Study Guide: **The Tragedy of Othello, the Moor of Venice***

LINE 165. *Would you have Othello threaten Emilia with the sword?*

ANSWER. Many students will say that Emilia is not responding to a threat but is merely expressing her determination to expose Othello. Others may have Othello point his sword at Emilia to emphasize his complete surrender to violence and irrationality.

LINE 197. *What are the possible meanings of Emilia's statement that she may "ne'er go home"?*

ANSWER. She may mean that she will refuse to remain Iago's wife, that she intends to kill herself "for grief," as she threatens in line 192, or that she may be prevented in some other way she cannot foresee.

LINE 198, STAGE DIRECTION. *Why does Othello fall on the bed here?*

ANSWER. Students may think that he is overcome with emotion or by the realization of the enormity of his deed or that he is starting to suspect that Iago deceived him.

LINE 200. *The stage direction calls for Othello to rise again. Why might Shakespeare have called for this action?*

ANSWER. Most students will agree that Othello rises when he has quieted his doubts and convinced himself again that Desdemona was guilty.

LINE 222. *In what tone of voice would you have Emilia deliver this speech?*

ANSWER. Many students would have Emilia speak loudly and urgently, to suggest both her anguish and her determination to be heard.

AFTER LINE 223, STAGE DIRECTION. *How would you interpret this instruction concerning Iago's movements?*

ANSWER. Many students will think that Iago advances toward Emilia with his sword drawn and is then stopped by Gratiano. Others may think that he makes a threatening gesture with his sword but does not move toward his wife.

AFTER LINE 235, STAGE DIRECTION. *In some productions, Othello does far more than merely run at Iago. One actor, for example, seized Iago by the throat, threw him to the floor, and put his foot on his neck. What action would you stage here?*

ANSWER. Students wishing to downplay the violence could have Iago deftly elude Othello's grasp, stab Emilia, and quickly run from the room.

LINE 243. *In what tone of voice would you have Montano give this speech? What role has he assumed?*

ANSWER. Most students will agree that Montano should speak rationally and authoritatively. He has assumed the role of civil authority, the person responsible for restoring public order.

LINE 246. *How has Othello's mood shifted?*

ANSWER. Othello is no longer angry with Iago but now blames himself and betrays a sense of having suffered an irretrievable loss.

LINE 258. *What does Othello want from Gratiano? What need do you think is driving Othello at this point?*

ANSWER. Othello wants to speak to Gratiano. Many students will suggest that Othello needs to explain or justify his killing of Desdemona.

LINE 271. *What is the effect of having Othello talk about himself in the third person?*

ANSWER. Many students will suggest that Othello's use of the third person gives the speech a self-dramatizing, self-pitying quality that diminishes the audience's sympathy for the protagonist.

LINE 281. *How would you have Othello move and speak as he confronts Desdemona's body?*

ANSWER. Some students may have Othello lift Desdemona's body, stare into her face, and then recoil as he cries out wildly "Whip me, ye devils."

AFTER LINE 286, STAGE DIRECTION. *In what manner would you have Othello attack Iago?*

ANSWER. Some students would have Othello attack Iago violently, with the intervention of the officers keeping another murder from occurring. Others would have Othello merely prod Iago to see whether he is a man (who will bleed) or an invulnerable devil.

LINE 292. *What attitude does Lodovico express toward Othello in this speech?*

ANSWER. Lodovico seems to express regret and amazement that such a good man could have allowed himself to be so misused by "a cursèd slave."

LINE 294. *According to this speech, how does Othello want his violence to be viewed? Do you think modern audiences can sympathize with his claim?*

Drama Study Guide: **The Tragedy of Othello, the Moor of Venice**

HRW MATERIAL COPYRIGHTED UNDER NOTICE APPEARING EARLIER IN THIS WORK.

53

ANSWER. Othello wants to be viewed as a rational man who acted not out of passion but out of a sense of justice and honor. Modern audiences with different views of honor will undoubtedly have difficulty sympathizing with Othello on these grounds.

? **LINE 303.** *How would you have Iago deliver his last speech?*

ANSWER. Most students will agree that Iago should speak coldly and implacably, showing little emotion other than contempt for all.

? **LINE 317.** *What part do these letters, presented by Lodovico, play in the resolution, or denouement, of the action?*

ANSWER. The letters provide the details of Iago's treachery and give Othello the opportunity to face the consequences of his actions.

? **LINE 336.** *How does Lodovico deal with Othello and Iago? What effect do you think Shakespeare intended these actions to create in the audience?*

ANSWER. Lodovico orders that Iago be imprisoned and tortured. He orders that Othello be removed from office and held until the Venetian authorities decide his fate. Shakespeare probably intended these actions to impart to the audience the feeling that justice has been served and order restored.

? **LINE 355.** *What effect on the audience would you want Othello's last speech to have?*

ANSWER. Most students would want the audience members to feel intense sadness and a sense of the tragic waste of life as they consider this man with great talent and a loving wife who allowed his happiness to be destroyed by evil forces.

? **AFTER LINE 355, STAGE DIRECTION.** *In some productions, Iago, who is present when Othello stabs himself, smiles. How would you have Iago react to Othello's death?*

ANSWER. Some students would want Iago to remain impassive and inscrutable, refusing to the last to remove the mask that hides his true feelings.

? **LINE 358.** *Some directors have omitted this speech and Othello's kissing Desdemona. How would you stage Othello's death?*

ANSWER. Some students may agree that the kiss is melodramatic, but most will want Othello to fall on the bed in order to underscore the couple's unity in life and in death.

? **LINE 360.** *How do you interpret Cassio's final judgment of Othello's character?*

ANSWER. Many students will suggest that Cassio's judgment echoes Othello's own self-evaluation in line 343—that he was essentially a passionate and loving man but not a wise or discerning one.

Drama Study Guide: **The Tragedy of Othello, the Moor of Venice**

54   HRW MATERIAL COPYRIGHTED UNDER NOTICE APPEARING EARLIER IN THIS WORK.

Graphic Organizer for Active Reading, Act I

How Are They Related?

In Act I, Shakespeare introduces the main characters in his tragedy and begins to reveal the nature of their relationships. As you read the act, note pairs of characters who are connected by blood, emotion, duty, or need. Write the names of these characters above the figures. Then, on the lines between them, summarize their apparent relationship. Finally, answer the questions that follow.

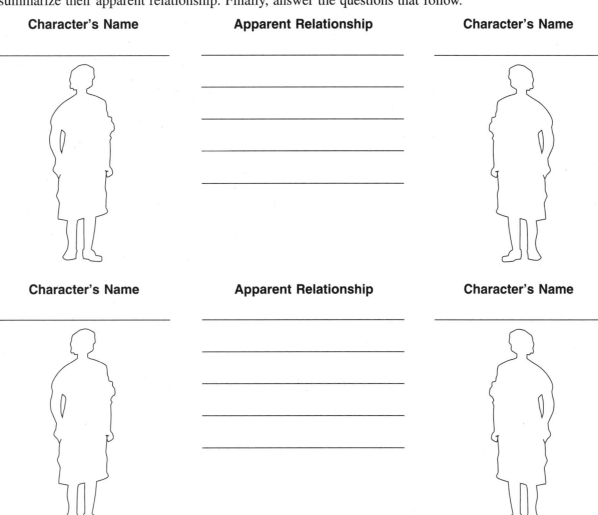

Character's Name	Apparent Relationship	Character's Name

Character's Name	Apparent Relationship	Character's Name

1. On the basis of what you know so far, choose one of the pairs of characters above whose actual relationship is different from their apparent one, and describe the difference between the appearance and the reality of their bond.

   _____

   _____

2. Which of these relationships do you predict will change during the play? Choose one relationship, and describe how you think it will change. Give one reason for your prediction.

   _____

   _____

*Drama Study Guide: **The Tragedy of Othello, the Moor of Venice***

HRW MATERIAL COPYRIGHTED UNDER NOTICE APPEARING EARLIER IN THIS WORK.

55

Making Meanings, Act I

First Thoughts

1. What kind of man does Othello seem to be? Would you want to put the safety of your country in his hands?

Shaping Interpretations

2. In Scene 1, Iago, Roderigo, and Brabantio all reveal their feelings about Othello. Why are Roderigo and Brabantio hostile toward him? How does Iago's hostility differ from that of the other two men?

3. How does Othello react to Brabantio's outrage over his marriage and to the argument between Iago and Roderigo in Scene 2? What do these actions reveal about Othello's **character**?

4. How does Othello characterize himself in his first address to the duke and the senators? Does his self-description seem accurate, from what you have seen and heard of him so far? Explain.

5. At the end of Scene 3, in lines 391–394, Iago ridicules Othello for believing that others are honest just because they appear to be so. Some people might agree with Othello's standard for judging the honesty of others. Do you agree with it? Why or why not?

6. In addition to learning about Othello from his own words and actions, we learn about him through the opinions of the other characters. What is the duke's and the senators' opinion of Othello? What does Iago say privately about Othello's character?

7. What account of his courtship of Desdemona does Othello give the senators? How does Desdemona describe her feelings for Othello when she asks to accompany him to Cyprus?

8. Although Iago and Roderigo share a hatred of Othello, they are **foils,** or opposites, in many ways. How are their differences revealed in their dialogue near the end of Scene 3?

9. Through Iago's **soliloquies**—the speeches he makes when he is alone onstage—we glimpse his true feelings and **motives.** What additional grievance against Othello does he reveal, and what plan does he hatch, at the end of Act I?

Challenging the Text

10. In Brabantio's view, Desdemona's love for Othello is unnatural, yet she asserts this love and acts on it. Why do you think Desdemona is attracted to Othello? Do you find their love believable as Shakespeare presents it?

Reviewing the Text

a. Why is Iago angry with Othello?

b. How does Iago plan to behave toward Othello?

c. Why is Brabantio upset about Desdemona's marriage to Othello?

d. How does Desdemona present her marriage to her father, the duke, and the senators?

e. What is Othello's opinion of Iago? How does Othello reveal this opinion in Scene 3?

---

*Drama Study Guide: **The Tragedy of Othello, the Moor of Venice***

Words to Own Worksheet, Act I

Developing Vocabulary

Carefully read the definition and explanation of each word and the sample sentence, which shows how the word can be used. Then, write a sentence using the word. In your sentence, include context clues that point to the word's meaning.

1. **obsequious** (əb·sē′kwē·əs) **adj.** too willing to obey; fawning; subservient. ▲ *Obsequious* comes from the Latin *sequi,* meaning "to follow."

   ■ The obsequious employee was always flattering her supervisor. (Scene 1, line 44)

   Original sentence: _____

   _____

2. **vexation** (vek·sā′shən) **n.** trouble, irritation. ▲ *Vexation* may refer to the state of being troubled or to the cause of the trouble.

   ■ Do you think the dripping faucet is a greater vexation than a mild case of poison ivy? (Scene 1, line 70)

   Original sentence: _____

   _____

3. **timorous** (tim′ər·əs) **adj.** fearful, timid. ▲ Shakespeare used the word to mean "frightening."

   ■ The timorous child quaked and shivered whenever the neighbor's dog growled and bared its teeth. (Scene 1, line 73)

   Original sentence: _____

   _____

4. **civility** (sə·vil′ə·tē) **n.** courtesy, politeness. ▲ *Civility* refers more to public conduct than to private conduct; the word comes from the Latin *civilis,* meaning "civil."

   ■ Many observers believe that there is no civility in today's down-and-dirty election campaigns. (Scene 1, line 128)

   Original sentence: _____

   _____

5. **iniquity** (in·ik′wə·tē) **n.** evildoing, wickedness. ▲ *Iniquity* denotes an offense against morality rather than a mere violation of law or custom.

   ■ The iniquity of Adolf Hitler continues to shock the world. (Scene 2, line 3)

   Original sentence: _____

   _____

(Continued on page 58.)

Drama Study Guide: The Tragedy of Othello, the Moor of Venice

(Continued from page 57.)

6. grievance (grē′vəns) *n.* complaint arising from a condition or situation thought to be unjust. ▲ Shakespeare used *grievance* to mean "punishment."

■ The tenants' main grievance was the lack of heat and hot water in the building. (Scene 2, line 14)

Original sentence: _____

_____

7. promulgate (präm′əl·gāt′) *v.* to make known by open declaration; to proclaim. ▲ *Promulgate* also means "to put into action or force."

■ Once the legislators promulgate the city's new curfew, no teenagers can claim that they didn't know they had to be off the streets by eleven o'clock. (Scene 2, line 20)

Original sentence: _____

_____

8. palpable (pal′pə·b'l) *adj.* capable of being touched or felt. ▲ The antonym is *impalpable.*

■ The healthy infant's heartbeat was palpable even without a stethoscope. (Scene 2, line 75)

Original sentence: _____

_____

9. facile (fas′'l) *adj.* easily accomplished or obtained. ▲ *Facile* can also mean "superficial" or "insincere."

■ The procedure was so facile that even beginners mastered it within an hour. (Scene 3, line 27)

Original sentence: _____

_____

10. imminent (im′ə·nənt) *adj.* ready to take place, about to occur. ▲ *Imminent* often suggests the approach of something threatening.

■ You could tell from the anvil-shaped cloud that a thunderstorm was imminent. (Scene 3, line 135)

Original sentence: _____

_____

Drama Study Guide: **The Tragedy of Othello, the Moor of Venice**

Literary Elements Worksheet, Act I

Irony

Irony is the contrast or discrepancy between expectation and reality—between what is said and what is really meant (**verbal irony**), between what is expected to happen by the audience or by a character and what really happens (**dramatic irony**), or between what appears to be true and what is true (**situational irony**).

Understanding Irony

As you re-read each passage cited below, decide which type of irony it reflects. Write *verbal, dramatic,* or *situational* on the line after each numbered passage. Then, briefly explain the discrepancy or the contrast that the passage reveals.

1. Scene 1, lines 104–105 ("Most grave Brabantio, / In simple and pure soul I come to you.")

_____

_____

2. Scene 2, lines 1–5 ("Though in the trade of war . . . under the ribs.")

_____

_____

3. Scene 3, lines 65–70 ("Whoe'er he be . . . stood in your action.")

_____

_____

4. Scene 3, lines 81–94 ("Rude am I in my speech. . . . I won his daughter—")

_____

_____

5. Scene 3, lines 94–98 ("A maiden never bold. . . to look on!")

_____

_____

6. Scene 3, lines 279–280 ("So please your grace, my ancient; / A man he is of honesty and trust.")

_____

_____

(Continued on page 60.)

Drama Study Guide: The Tragedy of Othello, the Moor of Venice

(Continued from page 59.)

Applying Skills

Considering the examples of irony you have just discussed, how do you see the theme of appearance versus reality emerging in the play? Which characters are having difficulty distinguishing between what seems to be true and what really is true, and who is manipulating appearances? Write your answer on the lines provided, and support it with specific evidence from the text.

_____

_____

_____

_____

_____

_____

_____

_____

Reader's Response

Do you think that Shakespeare's concern with the difficulty of distinguishing between appearance and reality is important? Is it relevant to your life? Can you think of real-life situations in which it was difficult to interpret another person's character, intentions, or motives? What makes it difficult to know another person well? Explain your responses.

_____

_____

_____

_____

_____

_____

_____

_____

*Drama Study Guide: **The Tragedy of Othello, the Moor of Venice***

NAME _____ CLASS _____ DATE _____ SCORE ____

Test, Act I

Thoughtful Reading *(40 points)*

On the line provided, write the letter of the best answer to each of the following items. *(8 points each)*

_____ 1. Iago's reaction to Othello's appointing Cassio to be his second in command is

    a. anger   **b.** joy   **c.** approval   **d.** indifference

_____ 2. Which of the following lines does *not* reflect Iago's strategy for dealing with Othello?

    a. "I follow him to serve my turn upon him."
    b. "In following him, I follow but myself."
    c. "I must show out a flag and sign of love / Which is indeed but sign."
    d. "Rouse him. Make after him, poison his delight."

_____ 3. What is the relationship between Iago and Roderigo?

    a. They are competitors for the favor of Othello.
    b. They are rivals for the affection of Desdemona.
    c. They are allies in a plot to harm Othello.
    d. They are true friends who confide completely in each other.

_____ 4. Brabantio accuses Othello of having "practiced on [Desdemona] with foul charms." Why does he make such an accusation?

    a. He cannot understand how his daughter could love a man of another race.
    b. His mind is unbalanced, and he is suspicious of everyone.
    c. He knows that Desdemona never met Othello before their elopement.
    d. The Venetian senate relies on Othello's knowledge of sorcery.

_____ 5. Which of the following lines from Act I is the *best* example of a *metaphor*?

    a. "The Moor is of a free and open nature."
    b. "And will as tenderly be led by the nose / As asses are."
    c. "Run from her guardage to the sooty bosom."
    d. "But I will wear my heart upon my sleeve / For daws to peck at."

Expanded Response *(30 points)*

6. Choose one of the following quotations from Act I. On the lines provided, write the letter of the quotation you choose, name the speaker, and discuss how the quotation reveals a conflict within the character and/or between that character and another. *(15 points)*

    a. "I know my price; I am worth no worse a place."
    b. "She is abused, stol'n from me, and corrupted."
    c. "I am hitherto your daughter. But here's my husband."
    d. "I will incontinently drown myself."

_____
_____
_____
_____

(Continued on page 62.)

Drama Study Guide: The Tragedy of Othello, the Moor of Venice

(Continued from page 61.)

7. In Act I, Othello's character is revealed by his words, his actions, and what other characters say about him. In the diagram below, fill in one example of each method of characterization, and explain what it suggests about Othello's character. *(15 points)*

Method of Characterization	Character Trait Revealed
Othello's Words	
Othello's Actions	
Others' Words About Othello	

Written Response *(30 points)*

8. Although Othello and Desdemona are happily married in Act I, there is a suggestion that their joy and security will not last. On a separate sheet of paper, write a paragraph explaining how Shakespeare introduces this sense of foreboding. Provide at least two examples from the play to support your answer.

_____

_____

_____

_____

_____

_____

_____

_____

_____

_____

_____

*Drama Study Guide: **The Tragedy of Othello, the Moor of Venice***

Graphic Organizer for Active Reading, Act II

Who Is Othello?

One way to learn about Othello is to listen to what other characters say about him and compare their views with his own words and actions. Use the cluster chart below to record other characters' opinions of Othello. In each character's oval, copy a passage about Othello spoken by that character in Act I or II. Then, answer the questions that follow.

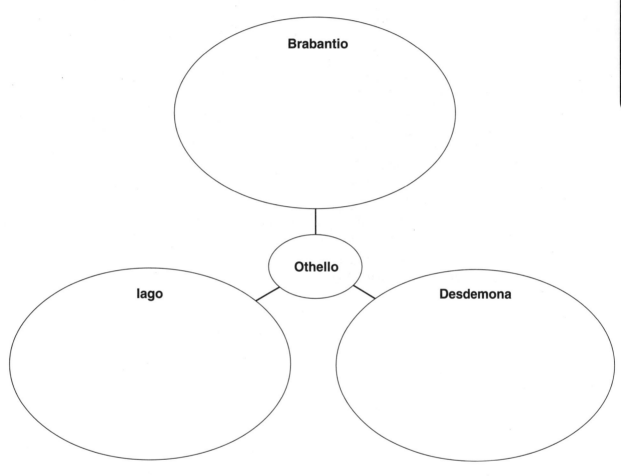

1. In Act II, Scene 3, lines 242–243, Othello says, "Cassio, I love thee; / But never more be officer of mine." What do these words and the action they refer to reveal about Othello's character?

   _____

   _____

2. Cite one action Othello takes in Act II that either supports or contradicts the opinion of him expressed by one of the characters in the diagram above.

   _____

   _____

Drama Study Guide: The Tragedy of Othello, the Moor of Venice

Making Meanings, Act II

First Thoughts

1. What was your response to Othello and Desdemona's reunion in Cyprus? What is Iago's response?

Shaping Interpretations

2. How does the **setting** change from Act I to Act II? What are some possible **symbolic** meanings of this change?

3. How does Cassio speak of Desdemona before she arrives from Venice? What does his greeting of her and Emilia reveal about his **character**?

4. Describe Iago's views of women as he expresses them to Desdemona in Scene 1 (lines 146–156). How does his language contrast with Cassio's when Cassio speaks of Desdemona (lines 61–65 and 74–82)?

Reviewing the Text

a. In the order of their appearance, list the characters who arrive from Venice in Scene 1.

b. What becomes of the Turkish threat?

c. What trouble does Iago stir up to disturb the peace of the island?

d. How does Othello react to the disturbance?

e. What advice does Iago give the remorseful Cassio?

---

5. Although Othello and Desdemona's reunion is joyful and passionate, the language of the scene hints at other emotions in Othello. Which lines could **foreshadow** trouble?

6. What emotion does Iago play on to get Roderigo to provoke Cassio? What weakness of Cassio's does Iago take advantage of? What do these actions reveal about Iago and his methods?

7. Iago often uses **imagery** of hell, darkness, disease, and traps when speaking of himself and his plots. Find instances of such images in his soliloquy at the end of Scene 3.

Extending the Text

8. Although most of the characters in the play are deceived, we in the audience know that Iago is a villain. Some critics see Iago as pure evil, whereas others say he is motivated by common human emotions. What do you think of Iago? Is he merely a stage villain, or are some people in the world very much like him? Explain your answer.

Challenging the Text

9. Some critics suggest that Othello, the career soldier who is used to action and physical deprivation, cannot tolerate prolonged intimacy and contentment and so must destroy his own happiness. What do you think of this remark? Do you think there is any evidence for this reading in the play so far?

Words to Own Worksheet, Act II

Developing Vocabulary

Carefully read the definition and explanation of each word and the sentence in the right-hand column, which shows how the word can be used. Then, write a sentence using the word. In your sentence, include context clues that point to the word's meaning.

ACT II

1. **discern** (di·surn′) *v.* to see, to recognize, or to notice. ▲ *Discern* also means "to distinguish with senses or mental processes other than vision."

   ■ From their teacher's frown the students could discern the disapproval. (Scene 1, line 1)

   Original sentence: _____

   _____

2. **citadel** (sit′ə·d'l) *n.* fortress set high above a city; stronghold. ▲ *Citadel* comes from the Latin *civitas,* meaning "citizenship."

   ■ The old citadel, perched high on a bluff above the city, must have provided excellent protection, for you could see an enemy approach from any direction. (Scene 1, line 94)

   Original sentence: _____

   _____

3. **discreet** (dis·krēt′) *adj.* having or showing good judgment about what one says or does. ▲ The quality of being *discreet* is expressed by the noun *discretion.* Both adjective and noun come from the Latin *cernere,* "to distinguish."

   ■ Because the family lawyer was so discreet about the will, no one but the old man's heirs ever learned the details. (Scene 1, line 221)

   Original sentence: _____

   _____

4. **eminent** (em′ə·nənt) *adj.* standing out so as to be easily noticed. ▲ *Eminent* is used more often to refer to outstanding quality than to refer to size or visibility. Do not confuse *eminent* with *imminent,* "approaching."

   ■ The eminent professor commanded the respect of all her colleagues. (Scene 1, line 233)

   Original sentence: _____

   _____

5. **impediment** (im·ped′ə·mənt) *n.* obstacle, bar, hindrance. ▲ A speech *impediment* obstructs the ability to speak clearly.

   ■ Lack of citizenship is an impediment to running for public office. (Scene 1, line 276)

   Original sentence: _____

   _____

(Continued on page 66.)

Drama Study Guide: The Tragedy of Othello, the Moor of Venice

(Continued from page 65.)

6. gnaw (nô) *v.* to bite or chew persistently.
▲ *Gnaw* can also mean "to wear away" or "to irritate."

■ His worries are always on his mind; they gnaw at him just as a hungry dog gnaws on a bone. (Scene 1, line 293)

Original sentence: _____

_____

7. ensue (in·sōō′) *v.* to take place after or as a result; to follow. ▲ In modern usage, *ensue* is almost always used intransitively, that is, without a direct object.

■ When lies and gossip are allowed to spread, trouble is sure to ensue. (Scene 3, line 9)

Original sentence: _____

_____

8. barbarous (bär′bər·əs) *adj.* uncivilized, cruel. ▲ The noun *barbarian* ("uncivilized or uncultured person") and the adjective *barbarous* come from the Greek word *barbaros* ("foreign, ignorant").

■ Their barbarous treatment of the cats prompted a visit from the Society for the Prevention of Cruelty to Animals. (Scene 3, line 166)

Original sentence: _____

_____

9. censure (sen′shər) *n.* strong disapproval; an official expression of disapproval.
▲ Shakespeare used the word to mean "judgment."

■ With its scathing editorial the newspaper's staff made sure the corrupt politician felt the censure of the press. (Scene 3, line 187)

Original sentence: _____

_____

10. inordinate (in·ôr′də·nit) *adj.* uncontrolled, excessive, exceeding reasonable limits.
▲ Antonyms of *inordinate* include *moderate* and *temperate.*

■ The vain youth spent an inordinate amount of time looking in the mirror. (Scene 3, line 300)

Original sentence: _____

_____

*Drama Study Guide: **The Tragedy of Othello, the Moor of Venice***

Literary Elements Worksheet, Act II

Imagery

Imagery is language that appeals to the senses (sight, hearing, smell, taste, touch). Throughout *Othello,* Shakespeare uses patterns of imagery, or repeated images, that reflect the characters, mood, and themes of the play.

Understanding Imagery

Re-read the following lines from the play, and identify the pattern or patterns of imagery in each passage. Then, answer the questions that follow each quotation.

1. "With as little a web as this will I ensnare as great a fly as Cassio." (Scene 1, lines 166–167)

   _____

   What does this imagery reveal about Iago's character? _____

   What other sentence in the passage extends this pattern of imagery? _____

   _____

2. "Her eye must be fed. And what delight shall she have to look on the devil?" (Scene 1, lines

   221–223) _____

   To whom does this passage refer? _____

   Who is being referred to as the devil in this passage? _____

3. "The thought whereof / Doth, like a poisonous mineral, gnaw my inwards. . . ." (Scene 1, lines

   292–293) _____

   What two things are being directly compared here?_____

   What other image of consumption is used by Iago in this passage? _____

   _____

4. "He'll be as full of quarrel and offense / As my young mistress' dog." (Scene 3, lines 46–47)

   _____

   Which character is being compared to a dog? _____

   Is the characterization borne out by events? Explain your answer. _____

   _____

5. "O thou invisible spirit of wine, if thou hast no name to be known by, let us call thee devil!" (Scene

   3, lines 275–277) _____

(Continued on page 68.)

Drama Study Guide: The Tragedy of Othello, the Moor of Venice

HRW MATERIAL COPYRIGHTED UNDER NOTICE APPEARING EARLIER IN THIS WORK.

67

(Continued from page 67.)

What two things are being equated in this image? _____

_____

What image in Act II complements or contradicts this one? Cite the passage. _____

_____

6. "I'll pour this pestilence into his ear. . . ." (Scene 3, line 347) _____

_____

Why might Iago repeatedly use this type of imagery? _____

_____

How does this imagery affect the mood of the scene? _____

_____

7. "So will I turn her virtue into pitch, / And out of her own goodness make the net / That shall en-

mesh them all." (Scene 3, lines 351–353) _____

_____

Which character is being described? _____

What passage earlier in the act does this one echo? _____

_____

Applying Skills

Choose one of the patterns of imagery that you identified above, and explain how it relates to one of the conflicts in the play. Consider the conflicts between civilization and barbarism, reason and instinct, and good and evil. Include additional images from the play to make your point.

_____

_____

_____

_____

_____

_____

_____

_____

*Drama Study Guide: **The Tragedy of Othello, the Moor of Venice***

Test, Act II

Thoughtful Reading *(40 points)*

On the line provided, write the letter of the *best* answer to each of the following items. *(8 points each)*

_____ 1. Which of the following is *not* true of Cassio's character?

    a. He is a ladies' man.
    b. He is loyal to Othello.
    c. He is always in control.
    d. He has a weakness for alcohol.

_____ 2. Iago urges Roderigo to provoke Cassio by telling him that

    a. Desdemona is now in love with Cassio
    b. Cassio has replaced Roderigo in Othello's favor
    c. Cassio has been wooing Iago's wife
    d. Cassio has injured Desdemona's reputation

_____ 3. Which of the following characters are *foils,* or opposites?

    a. Iago and Emilia
    b. Iago and Cassio
    c. Desdemona and Cassio
    d. Othello and Cassio

_____ 4. In Scene 3, Othello becomes angry with Cassio because

    a. Cassio has been flirting with Desdemona
    b. Cassio refuses to obey Othello's orders
    c. while supervising the watch, Cassio got into a fight
    d. he is jealous of Cassio's popularity with the local gentlemen

_____ 5. What step in his plan to entrap the main characters does Iago take at the end of Act II?

    a. He urges Cassio to seek Desdemona's help in getting his position back.
    b. He convinces Othello that Desdemona has been unfaithful.
    c. He gets Roderigo to pick a fight with Cassio.
    d. He persuades Cassio to drink too much while on duty.

Expanded Response *(30 points)*

6. Choose one of the following quotations from Act II. On the lines provided, write the letter of the quotation you choose, name the speaker, and discuss how the quotation reveals the speaker's character. Use at least one example from the play to support your ideas. *(15 points)*

    a. "For I am nothing if not critical."
    b. "I am not merry; but I do beguile / The thing I am."
    c. "I cannot speak enough of this content; / It stops me here; it is too much of joy."
    d. "Reputation, reputation, reputation! O, I have lost my reputation! I have lost the immortal part of myself, and what remains is bestial."

_____

_____

_____

_____

_____

(Continued on page 70.)

*Drama Study Guide: **The Tragedy of Othello, the Moor of Venice***

(Continued from page 69.)

7. In Act II, Shakespeare reveals more of the characters' emotions and shows how their emotions influence their actions. In the second column of the diagram below, fill in the name of a character who displays the emotion named in the first column. Then, in the third column, give one example of how the character has acted on his or her emotion, quoting lines from the play if you can. *(15 points)*

Emotion	Character	Action Based on Emotion
anger		
love		
envy		

Written Response *(30 points)*

8. In his soliloquies in Acts I and II, Iago reveals his plan to destroy Othello. Re-read these speeches and Iago's dialogues with Roderigo. Then, on the lines below, explain Iago's strategy and the steps he has taken so far to achieve his goal. Use at least two examples from the play to support your ideas.

_____

_____

_____

_____

_____

_____

_____

_____

_____

_____

_____

_____

_____

Drama Study Guide: **The Tragedy of Othello, the Moor of Venice**

Graphic Organizer for Active Reading, Act III

Weighing the Evidence

In Act III, Iago suggests to Othello that Desdemona and Cassio are lovers. Othello is immediately troubled and suspicious but demands that Iago furnish proof of Desdemona's betrayal. Iago then begins giving Othello "proof." On the left-hand scale below, list the evidence that Iago offers. On the right-hand scale, write your objective evaluation of this evidence as a juror or any other impartial person would do. Then, answer the questions that follow.

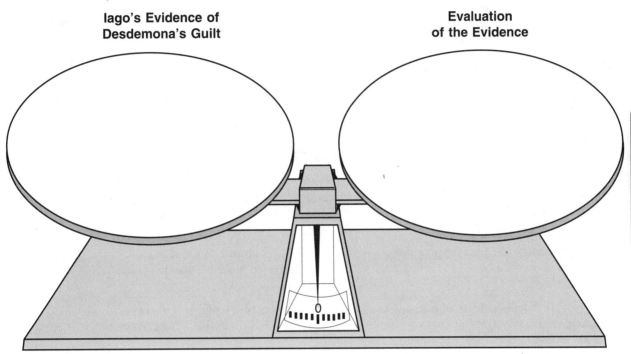

Iago's Evidence of Desdemona's Guilt

Evaluation of the Evidence

ACT III

1. Do you think Iago proved that Desdemona and Cassio are secretly betraying Othello? Why or why not?

   _____

   _____

   _____

   _____

2. Why might Othello have been so unsettled by Iago's charges against Desdemona? What does his behavior reveal about his character and the quality of his love for Desdemona?

   _____

   _____

   _____

   _____

*Drama Study Guide: **The Tragedy of Othello, the Moor of Venice***

Making Meanings, Act III

First Thoughts

1. What do you think of Othello when he begins to doubt Desdemona's faithfulness?

Shaping Interpretations

2. Scene 3 is often referred to as the temptation scene, in which Iago, like Satan, misleads Othello. What are some of the techniques Iago uses to plant suspicion in Othello's mind?

3. What emotion does Iago warn Othello against? What **irony** do you sense in his warning?

4. What contradictory feelings toward Desdemona does Othello express in Scene 3? What contrasting images does Othello use to reveal his confusion?

Reviewing the Text

a. How does Desdemona try to help Cassio?

b. What event in Scene 3 does Iago use to stir up Othello's doubts about Cassio?

c. What happens in Act III to the handkerchief Desdemona tries to use to soothe Othello?

d. What does the tortured Othello demand of Iago?

e. Which characters lie knowingly in Act III, and about what?

5. In the course of Scene 3, Othello admires, trusts, doubts, makes demands of, and gets angry with Iago. How would you describe the relationship between Othello and Iago by the scene's end?

6. Key **themes** of the play involve the passions of love and jealousy. Who besides Othello shows jealousy of a loved one? What other forms of jealousy are displayed in the play?

7. In Act III, Scene 3, Iago admits to Othello that "it is my nature's plague / To spy into abuses, and of my jealousy / Shapes faults that are not" (lines 146–148). What does this say about how our imaginations work?

8. In Act III, Scene 3, Iago's metaphor compares jealousy to "the green-eyed monster which doth mock / The meat it feeds on" (lines 166–167). Why is this a fitting description of a jealous person?

Extending the Text

9. In the play, jealousy is often referred to as a monster or a disease that destroys the lover and the beloved. What other figure of speech could you use to describe jealousy between lovers?

Challenging the Text

10. Othello is finally convinced of Desdemona's guilt when Iago says that he saw Cassio with the handkerchief and then Desdemona denies losing it. Has Shakespeare given Othello sufficient motivation for his jealousy, or is the slender evidence on which he acts a flaw in the play's construction? Explain your answer.

Words to Own Worksheet, Act III

Developing Vocabulary

Carefully read the definition and explanation of each word and the sentence in the right-hand column, which shows how the word can be used. Then, write a sentence using the word. In your sentence, include context clues that point to the word's meaning.

1. **procure** (prō·kyoor′) *v.* to get possession of, to obtain through care or effort. ▲ *Procure* is formed from the Latin prefix *pro-* ("for") and the verb *curare* ("to attend to").

■ After going through numerous channels, the sergeant was able to procure extra rations for his soldiers. (Scene 1, line 33)

Original sentence: _____

_____

2. **affinity** (ə·fin′ə·tē) *n.* familial relationship, kinship. ▲ *Affinity* also means "sympathy" or "attraction based on similarity."

■ Indeed, there is an affinity between us: She is my mother's first cousin's sister-in-law. (Scene 1, line 43)

Original sentence: _____

_____

3. **penitent** (pen′ə·tənt) *adj.* feeling sorrow for having committed a wrongdoing; repentant. ▲ As a noun, *penitent* means "a person who is sorry or who repents."

■ Because the defendant was penitent and apologized to the victim, the judge gave her a lenient sentence. (Scene 3, line 63)

Original sentence: _____

_____

4. **ruminate** (roo′mə·nāt′) *v.* to go over and over in one's mind. ▲ *Ruminate* also means "to chew repeatedly."

■ My cousin makes snap decisions, whereas I ruminate for days before I make up my mind. (Scene 3, line 132)

Original sentence: _____

_____

5. **inference** (in′fər·əns) *n.* a conclusion based on some facts or evidence. ▲ Shakespeare used *inference* to mean "allegation; depiction."

■ The public can make an inference about a case based on the evidence, but a prosecutor must prove beyond a reasonable doubt that such a conclusion is valid. (Scene 3, line 183)

Original sentence: _____

_____

ACT III

(Continued on page 74.)

Drama Study Guide: The Tragedy of Othello, the Moor of Venice

(Continued from page 73.)

6. **disposition** (dis′pə·zish′ən) *n.* the orderly arrangement or settlement of a matter. ▲ Shakespeare used *disposition* to mean "prevailing tendency," "mood," or "temperament."

■ The disposition of the case will come as a relief, for it has been unsettled and chaotic for years. (Scene 3, line 201)

Original sentence: _____

_____

7. **vehement** (vē′ə·mənt) *adj.* powerful, strongly felt or expressed. ▲ *Vehement,* like *vehemence* ("forceful expression"), is from the Latin *vehemens* ("eager").

■ The senator's opposition to the proposed legislation was so vehement that there was no doubting where she stood. (Scene 3, line 251)

Original sentence: _____

_____

8. **tranquil** (traŋ′kwəl) *adj.* free from disturbance; calm; quiet. ▲ *Tranquil, tranquillity* ("a peaceful state"), and *tranquilize* ("to make calm") are all from the Latin *tranquillus* ("calm").

■ Once the wind died down and the sun came out, the lake returned to its tranquil state. (Scene 3, line 345)

Original sentence: _____

_____

9. **compulsive** (kəm·pul′siv) *adj.* having to do with irresistible force. ▲ *Compulsive* is a term often used in psychology.

■ His house is extremely neat because he is compulsive about putting everything in its place. (Scene 3, line 451)

Original sentence: _____

_____

10. **loathed** (lō*th*d) *v.* disliked intensely, often with disgust; hated. ▲ A related adjective is *loath,* meaning "unwilling or reluctant to do something."

■ We loathed the chartreuse suit that had hung on the rack for months, shunned by every customer who entered the store. (Scene 4, line 68)

Original sentence: _____

_____

*Drama Study Guide: **The Tragedy of Othello, the Moor of Venice***

Literary Elements Worksheet, Act III

Conflict

Conflict is a struggle between opposing characters, forces, or emotions. In an **external conflict** a character struggles against an outside force, such as another character, society, or nature. In an **internal conflict** opposing feelings, desires, or beliefs are contending within a single character.

Understanding Conflict

As you re-read each passage listed below, decide whether it reflects an internal or an external conflict. After each numbered passage, write the name of the character(s) whose conflict the passage refers to, the nature of the conflict (internal or external), and the opposing forces.

1. Scene 3, lines 60–89 ("Why, then, tomorrow night . . . To leave me but a little to myself.")

_____

_____

2. Scene 3, lines 257–276 ("This fellow's of exceeding honesty. . . . When we do quicken.")

_____

_____

3. Scene 3, lines 356–380 ("Villain, be sure thou prove my love a whore! . . . And loses that it works

for.") _____

_____

4. Scene 3, lines 380–387 ("By the world . . . Would I were satisfied!") _____

_____

5. Scene 3, lines 425–428 ("But this denoted a foregone conclusion. . . . I'll tear her all to pieces!")

_____

_____

6. Scene 4, lines 53–99 ("Lend me thy handkerchief. . . . Away!") _____

_____

7. Scene 4, 141–155 ("Something sure of state . . . And he's indicted falsely.") _____

_____

8. Scene 4, lines 180–196 ("Take me this work out. . . . But that you do not love me!")

_____

_____

(Continued on page 76.)

ACT III

*Drama Study Guide: **The Tragedy of Othello, the Moor of Venice***

HRW MATERIAL COPYRIGHTED UNDER NOTICE APPEARING EARLIER IN THIS WORK.

75

(Continued from page 75.)

Applying Skills

Considering the conflicts you have identified above, especially the internal conflicts, what do you see as the emerging theme of the play? Give specific reasons for your answer, citing evidence from the text.

_____

_____

_____

_____

_____

_____

_____

_____

_____

_____

Reader's Response

What do you think of Iago's effort to stir up jealousy in Othello? Think about what drives his behavior. Is he consumed by jealousy, envy, or desire for revenge? Does he simply get pleasure out of destroying the happiness of others? Do you think he wants to prove his personal power or superior intelligence?

_____

_____

_____

_____

_____

_____

_____

_____

_____

*Drama Study Guide: **The Tragedy of Othello, the Moor of Venice***

Test, Act III

Thoughtful Reading *(40 points)*

On the line provided, write the letter of the *best* answer to each of the following items. *(8 points each)*

_____ 1. Cassio's referring to Iago as "kind and honest" in Scene 1 is an example of

    a. figurative language   **c.** situational irony
    b. exaggeration   **d.** dramatic irony

_____ 2. Iago urges Cassio to seek Desdemona's help in getting his position back because

    a. Iago wants to win Cassio's allegiance
    b. Iago wants Othello to see Cassio and Desdemona talking privately
    c. Iago believes that Desdemona will be unwilling to help Cassio
    d. Iago is afraid of talking to Othello directly about Cassio

_____ 3. In a famous metaphor in Scene 3, Iago compares jealousy to

    a. the green-eyed monster   **c.** the vapor of a dungeon
    b. the plague to great ones   **d.** trifles light as air

_____ 4. How does Iago obtain possession of Desdemona's handkerchief?

    a. He steals it from Desdemona's room.
    b. Desdemona gives it to him as a token of her love.
    c. Emilia finds it and gives it to Iago.
    d. Emilia steals it at Iago's request.

_____ 5. What does Desdemona lie about in Scene 4?

    a. She tells Othello that she does not love Cassio.
    b. She tells Emilia that she does not believe Othello is jealous.
    c. She claims she still has the handkerchief when she knows she has lost it.
    d. She pretends to love Othello.

Expanded Response *(30 points)*

6. Which of the following quotations do you think best describes the *theme* of Act III? Choose the quotation that accurately communicates the central message. On the lines provided, write the letter of the quotation you choose, and briefly defend your choice. There is more than one possible answer. Give at least one reason based on the text to support your choice. *(15 points)*

    a. "But I do love thee! and when I love thee not, / Chaos is come again."
    b. "Good name in man and woman . . . , / Is the immediate jewel of their souls."
    c. "Away at once with love or jealousy!"
    d. "O, beware my lord of jealousy! / It is the green-eyed monster which doth mock / The meat it feeds on."

_____

_____

_____

_____

(Continued on page 78.)

*Drama Study Guide: **The Tragedy of Othello, the Moor of Venice***

(Continued from page 77.)

7. Three characters in Act III are taken in or fooled by Iago. None recognizes Iago's true aims or motives. On the diagram below, name the three characters, and give at least one example of how each one is duped by Iago. *(15 points)*

Name of Character	How Iago Fools Him or Her

Written Response *(30 points)*

8. Why do you think Desdemona persists in pleading Cassio's case even after it becomes obvious that her entreaties annoy her husband? At least one critic has suggested that she may have been in love with Cassio. What do you think is her motivation? On the lines below, give your opinion, citing at least two references from the play to support your view.

_____

_____

_____

_____

_____

_____

_____

_____

_____

_____

_____

*Drama Study Guide: **The Tragedy of Othello, the Moor of Venice***

Graphic Organizer for Active Reading, Act IV

A Study in Contrasts

Emilia and Desdemona are **foils,** characters who set off each other's personalities by virtue of their obvious differences. The contrast brings out the distinctive qualities of each character and often highlights an important way in which they are alike. Complete the Venn diagram below to show the ways in which Emilia and Desdemona are opposites and one important way in which they are alike. Then, answer the questions that follow.

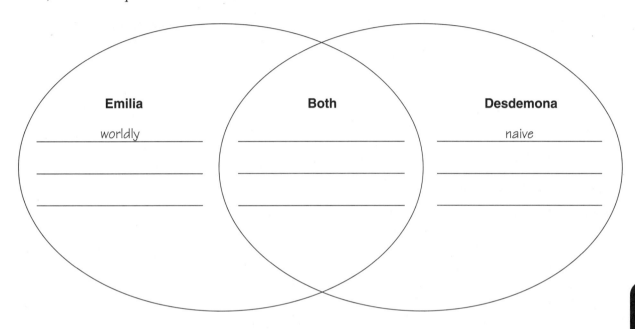

Emilia

worldly

_____

_____

Both

_____

_____

_____

Desdemona

naive

_____

_____

ACT IV

1. What do you think is more important—the similarities or the differences between the two women? Explain your response.

_____

_____

_____

_____

_____

2. What other pairs of characters in Act IV could be considered foils? Choose one pair, and describe how the two are a study in contrasts.

_____

_____

_____

_____

_____

*Drama Study Guide: **The Tragedy of Othello, the Moor of Venice***

Making Meanings, Act IV

First Thoughts

1. What do you think of Othello by the end of Act IV? How has he changed?

Shaping Interpretations

2. In Scene 1, Othello falls into an epileptic trance and Iago repeatedly refers to illness and madness. Find examples of these references. How do they emphasize and explain the change in Othello?

3. In this act there is a noticeable increase in **images** of animals, especially in Othello's speech and in references to Othello. (Earlier in the play, animal imagery was usually associated with Iago.) Find examples of this imagery in Act IV. What do these images say about Othello's state of mind?

4. How does Othello's brutality toward Desdemona contrast with his behavior earlier in the play?

5. How would you describe Othello's state of mind in Scene 2, when he speaks to Emilia and Desdemona in private? How does he respond to Desdemona's expressions of innocence?

6. The scene between Desdemona, Emilia, and Iago after Othello has spoken so brutally to his wife is full of **dramatic irony.** What does the audience know that these characters do not know?

7. In the final scene, how does Emilia function as a **foil,** or contrast, to Desdemona?

Reviewing the Text

a. What events does Othello interpret as proof that Desdemona and Cassio are having an affair?

b. What does Iago advise Othello to do to punish Desdemona? What is Othello's reaction?

c. What news does Lodovico bring from Venice?

d. Why is Roderigo impatient? How does Iago pacify him?

e. What questions does Desdemona ask Emilia when they are alone in the final scene of this act?

Connecting with the Text

8. How do you feel toward Desdemona when she sings her sad song and when she asks Emilia to shroud her in her wedding sheets?

Extending the Text

9. Desdemona is shocked and saddened by Othello's accusations. In what other ways might an innocent wife respond to a jealous husband's false accusations? How do you think Emilia would have behaved if her husband had accused her of infidelity?

*Drama Study Guide: **The Tragedy of Othello, the Moor of Venice***

Words to Own Worksheet, Act IV

Developing Vocabulary

Carefully read the definition and explanation of each word and the sentence in the right-hand column, which shows how the word can be used. Then, write a sentence using the word. In your sentence, include context clues that point to the word's meaning.

1. **dotage** (dōt′ij) *n.* state of mental decline associated with advanced age. ▲ Shakespeare used *dotage* to mean "infatuation."

   ■ Despite their advanced age, the sisters were not in their dotage—they were spry and sharp. (Scene 1, line 27)

   Original sentence: _____

   _____

2. **credulous** (krej′o͞o·ləs) *adj.* ready to believe, often on slight or uncertain evidence. ▲ The antonym of *credulous* is *incredulous,* meaning "unwilling to believe."

   ■ The dishonest contractor easily cheated the credulous homeowner. (Scene 1, line 46)

   Original sentence: _____

   _____

3. **lethargy** (leth′ər·jē) *n.* the quality or state of being drowsy, lazy, or indifferent. ▲ Shakespeare used *lethargy* to refer to a coma.

   ■ Because of my lethargy, I didn't move from the couch all afternoon. (Scene 1, line 54)

   Original sentence: _____

   _____

4. **beguile** (bi·gīl′) *v.* to deceive or to trick. ▲ *Beguile* can also mean "to pass time pleasantly."

   ■ The actors' smiles and good manners served to beguile the members of the audience, for they had no idea who was actually the villain. (Scene 1, line 98)

   Original sentence: _____

   _____

5. **importunes** (im′pôr·to͞onz′) *v.* begs or urges persistently. ▲ *Importune* often implies asking with troubling or annoying persistence.

   ■ The child daily importunes her father to take her swimming, and eventually he gives in to her requests. (Scene 1, line 114)

   Original sentence: _____

   _____

ACT IV

(Continued on page 82.)

*Drama Study Guide: **The Tragedy of Othello, the Moor of Venice***

(Continued from page 81.)

6. breach (brēch) *n.* break, rupture, or gap (either physical or social). ▲ As a verb, *breach* means "to break" or "to violate."

■ Failing to pay your share of the expenses was a breach of our agreement. (Scene 1, line 221)

Original sentence: _____

_____

7. requite (ri·kwīt′) *v.* to make suitable return for; to repay. ▲ To *requite* can imply returning injury for injury or benefit for benefit.

■ She will requite his generosity with a special gift of her own. (Scene 2, line 16)

Original sentence: _____

_____

8. impudent (im′pyo͞o·dənt) *adj.* shamelessly bold; cocky. ▲ Do not confuse *impudent* with *imprudent,* meaning "unwise" or "without proper thought or care."

■ The impudent passenger pushed ahead of three others to get the last seat on the bus. (Scene 2, line 80)

Original sentence: _____

_____

9. shroud (shroud) *v.* to screen, to veil, or to disguise. ▲ Shakespeare uses *shroud* to mean "to wrap in a burial garment."

■ In coastal areas, fog and mist often shroud the roads in the morning, markedly decreasing visibility. (Scene 3, line 25)

Original sentence: _____

_____

10. peevish (pē′vish) *adj.* whining; fretful; complaining. ▲ *Peevish* may derive from the Middle English word *pevish,* meaning "spiteful."

■ The peevish toddler refused to eat lunch or take a nap. (Scene 3, line 89)

Original sentence: _____

_____

Drama Study Guide: ***The Tragedy of Othello, the Moor of Venice***

Literary Elements Worksheet, Act IV

Atmosphere

Atmosphere is the mood or feeling of a literary work. The author creates the atmosphere or mood with descriptive details, the language, and the images. The atmosphere may change over the course of a work.

Understanding Atmosphere

Re-read each of the passages listed below. On the lines provided, describe how each passage makes you feel. Then, explain what details, words, or images contributed to your response.

1. Scene 1, lines 45–48 ("Work on. . . . All guiltless, meet reproach.")

_____

_____

_____

2. Scene 1, lines 179–188 ("Ay, let her rot. . . . Of so high and plenteous wit and invention—")

_____

_____

_____

3. Scene 1, line 197 ("I will chop her into messes! Cuckold me!")

_____

_____

_____

4. Scene 1, lines 204–209 ("Do it not with poison. . . . Excellent good!")

_____

_____

_____

5. Scene 1, lines 230–236 ("What, is he angry? . . . I have not deserved this.")

_____

_____

_____

ACT IV

(Continued on page 84.)

*Drama Study Guide: **The Tragedy of Othello, the Moor of Venice***

(Continued from page 83.)

6. Scene 1, lines 259–263 ("Is this the noble Moor . . . Could neither graze nor pierce?")

_____

_____

_____

7. Scene 2, lines 12–19 ("I durst, my lord . . . Is foul as slander.")

_____

_____

_____

8. Scene 2, lines 46–63 ("Had it pleased heaven . . . I here look grim as hell!")

_____

_____

_____

9. Scene 2, lines 100–105 ("Who is thy lord? . . . And call thy husband hither.")

_____

_____

10. Scene 3, lines 18–25 ("I would you had never seen him! . . . In one of these same sheets.")

_____

_____

_____

Applying Skills

Considering the feelings and the moods you have named above, what do you see as the predominant atmosphere of Act IV, and how does it compare or contrast with the prevailing atmosphere of the previous acts? Give specific reasons for your answer, citing evidence from the text.

_____

_____

_____

_____

_____

Drama Study Guide: ***The Tragedy of Othello, the Moor of Venice***

Test, Act IV

Thoughtful Reading *(40 points)*

On the line provided, write the letter of the *best* answer to each of the following items. *(8 points each)*

_____ **1.** Which of the following events convinces Othello that Desdemona has betrayed him?
   a. Cassio steals away when Othello approaches.
   b. Emilia supports Iago's accusations.
   c. Bianca gives Desdemona's handkerchief to Cassio.
   d. Desdemona denies that she has been unfaithful.

_____ **2.** How does Othello react when Iago suggests that he strangle Desdemona in her bed?
   a. He is horrified.
   b. He sees it as a just and fitting punishment.
   c. He is moved to pity the defenseless Desdemona.
   d. He fears he will not have the nerve to kill her.

_____ **3.** The increased use of animal imagery by Othello in Act IV reflects his
   a. loss of reason   **c.** nostalgia for his childhood
   b. rejection of Iago   **d.** injured pride

_____ **4.** Desdemona's request that she be shrouded in her wedding sheets if she should die is an example of
   a. paradox   **b.** metaphor   **c.** suspense   **d.** foreshadowing

_____ **5.** Which of the following adjectives does *not* describe Desdemona in the final scene with Emilia?
   a. worldly   **b.** innocent   **c.** idealistic   **d.** confused

Expanded Response *(30 points)*

6. Which of the following phrases do you think *best* describes Othello's state of mind when he talks to Desdemona in Scene 2? On the lines provided, write the letter of the answer you choose, and briefly defend your choice. There is more than one possible answer. Use at least one example from the play to support your choice. *(15 points)*

   a. in a jealous rage   **c.** coldly cruel
   b. disillusioned and humiliated   **d.** full of self-pity

_____

_____

_____

_____

_____

_____

(Continued on page 86.)

ACT IV

(Continued from page 85.)

7. Lodovico is shocked by the change in Othello and hardly recognizes him as the same self-confident, disciplined, and loving man he used to know. In the chart below, give examples of Othello's words and actions in Acts I–III that contrast with his behavior in Act IV. *(15 points)*

Characteristic of Othello	Acts I, II, and III	Act IV
self-confidence		
loving		
self-control		

Written Response *(30 points)*

8. Do you think Shakespeare intended the audience to have any sympathy for Othello in Scene 3, when the Moor disregards both Emilia's and Desdemona's assurances that Desdemona has done him no wrong? On the lines below, write a paragraph in which you give your opinion of this question, citing at least two references from the play to support your view.

_____

_____

_____

_____

_____

_____

_____

_____

_____

_____

_____

_____

_____

*Drama Study Guide: **The Tragedy of Othello, the Moor of Venice***

Graphic Organizer for Active Reading, Act V

Mapping the Action

In the beginning of a Shakespearean tragedy, there is a period in which the hero enjoys good fortune or personal happiness. This **rising action** is followed by a **turning point,** or crisis, usually in the third act, when something happens that causes the hero's fortunes to reverse. The action from now on is called **falling action,** because events grow worse and worse, until a **climax,** or point of great emotional intensity, is reached, usually in the last act. This climax is the moment when the conflict is decided once and for all and the hero cannot turn back. Following the climax is the **resolution,** when all the strands of the story are tied together and the fate of all the characters is made clear.

On the diagram below, indicate the path of the tragic action in *Othello* by filling in appropriate act and scene numbers on the lines provided. Then, answer the questions that follow.

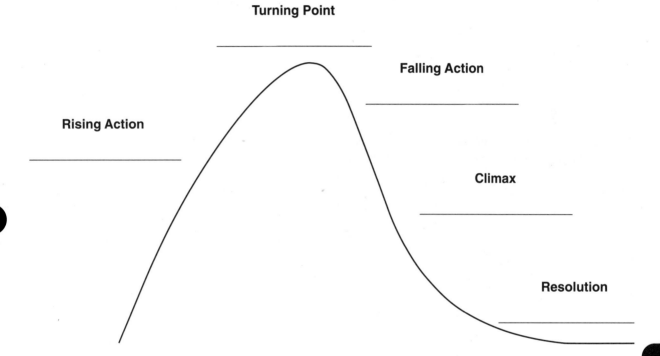

1. What event did you choose as the climax of *Othello*? Explain the reasons for your choice.

   _____

   _____

   _____

2. Did you find the resolution of *Othello* satisfactory? Why or why not?

   _____

   _____

   _____

*Drama Study Guide: **The Tragedy of Othello, the Moor of Venice***

Making Meanings, Act V

First Thoughts

1. Were you surprised by "the tragic loading of this bed" that occurs by the end of Act V? Which characters did you expect to die, and which did you expect to live?

Shaping Interpretations

2. **Imagery** of darkness and light pervade the play and especially the final act. Describe the **setting** of Scene 1. What could this setting **symbolize**?

3. For what practical reason does Iago want Cassio dead? What additional psychological **motive** does Iago reveal in Scene 1 for wanting to get rid of Cassio?

4. In trying to cast suspicion for Roderigo's death on Bianca, Iago uses a technique that he has relied on throughout the play. What is it?

Reviewing the Text

a. Who dies on the street in Venice, and by whose hand?

b. What does Iago pretend in the presence of Gratiano and Lodovico?

c. Who exposes Iago, and what happens when his treachery is revealed?

d. Before she dies, who does Desdemona say killed her?

e. What does Othello ask of Lodovico before killing himself?

---

5. Find images of light and dark in Othello's first speech in Scene 2 (lines 1–22). How do these contradictory images work to show us Othello's state of mind?

6. What are some of the elements of a love scene in Scene 2? In Othello's first speech in this scene (lines 1–22), he links the **themes** of love and death. This is especially obvious in lines 13–15 and 18–22. What effect does this have?

7. What contrasting **images** does Emilia use to condemn Othello and praise Desdemona when Othello confesses that he has killed his wife?

Connecting with the Text

8. Critics have debated whether or not Othello recovers his former noble stature at the end of the play, after he realizes that he has been duped by Iago and that his wife was innocent. What did you think of Othello as he turned his sword upon himself?

Extending the Text

9. Lodovico, speaking for the law-abiding citizens of Venice, has the last lines in the play. He expresses horror at Iago's villainy and a desire to hide the bloody scene from public view. How would today's audiences react to such a scene?

Words to Own Worksheet, Act V

Developing Vocabulary

Carefully read the definition and explanation of each word and the sentence in the right-hand column, which shows how the word can be used. Then, write a sentence using the word. In your sentence, include context clues that point to the word's meaning.

1. restitution (res′tə·tōō′shən) *n.* an act of restoring or making good. ▲ *Restitution,* like the verb· *restitute* ("to restore"), is from the Latin verb *restituere* ("to set up again").

■ She promised the landlord that she would make financial <u>restitution</u> for the couch her cat destroyed. (Scene 1, line 15)

Original sentence: _____

_____

2. monumental (män′yə·men′t′l) *adj.* serving or resembling a monument or a memorial. ▲ *Monumental* also means "massive," "outstanding," "great."

■ At first many people believed that Maya Lin's design for the Vietnam Veterans Memorial was not suitably <u>monumental</u>. (Scene 2, line 5)

Original sentence: _____

_____

3. quench (kwench) *v.* to put out (as fire or light). ▲ *Quench* also means "to satisfy or relieve (a physical or emotional need)."

■ The firefighters are trying to <u>quench</u> the raging flames with water from the hydrant. (Scene 2, line 8)

Original sentence: _____

_____

4. portents (pôr′tents) *n. pl.* things that fore-shadow a coming event. ▲ *Portent,* like the verb *portend* ("to give a sign of what is to come"), is from the Latin verb *portendere* ("to stretch through").

■ Some people believe that black cats crossing your path are <u>portents</u> of trouble. (Scene 2, line 45)

Original sentence: _____

_____

5. pernicious (pər·nish′əs) *adj.* very destructive; deadly. ▲ An older or archaic meaning of *pernicious* is "wicked" or "evil."

■ The <u>pernicious</u> virus leaves its victims dangerously weakened. (Scene 2, line 155)

Original sentence: _____

_____

(Continued on page 90.)

ACT V

*Drama Study Guide: **The Tragedy of Othello, the Moor of Venice***

(Continued from page 89.)

6. amorous (am′ər·əs) *adj.* having to do with love. ▲ *Amorous* comes from the Latin noun *amor* ("love") and the verb *amare* ("to love").

■ Every day the love-struck teenager wrote an amorous letter to his absent girlfriend. (Scene 2, line 213)

Original sentence: _____

_____

7. viper (vī′pər) *n.* poisonous snake. ▲ *Viper* can also refer to a vicious and destructive person.

■ The viper slithered through the grass and, true to form, hissed with its forked tongue. (Scene 2, line 284)

Original sentence: _____

_____

8. wrench (rench) *v.* to twist violently or take forcibly. ▲ As a noun, a *wrench* is a forceful pull or twist or a tool for twisting.

■ The strong woman was able to wrench the top off the jar of spaghetti sauce. (Scene 2, line 287)

Original sentence: _____

_____

9. ensnared (in·snerd′) *v.* trapped, caught. ▲ *Ensnared* can also mean "taken in or fooled by tricks or strategies."

■ The lepidopterist ensnared the butterfly in his net. (Scene 2, line 301)

Original sentence: _____

_____

10. interim (in′tər·im) *n.* time between; interval. ▲ *Interim* comes from the Latin adverb *interim,* which means "meanwhile."

■ What will you do during the interim between school and work? (Scene 2, line 316)

Original sentence: _____

_____

*Drama Study Guide: **The Tragedy of Othello, the Moor of Venice***

Literary Elements Worksheet, Act V

Tragedy

Tragedy is a type of drama that depicts serious and important events that end unhappily for the main character. This main character, or **tragic hero,** is usually dignified, courageous, and of high rank. His downfall may be caused by a **tragic flaw**—an error in judgment or a personal weakness—or it may result from natural or supernatural forces beyond his control. The tragic hero usually gains some wisdom or self-knowledge as a result of his suffering.

Understanding Tragedy

Illustrate each of the following characteristics of tragedy by quoting a passage or summarizing an event from Act V of *Othello*. Then, give a brief explanation of how the quote or the summary represents an aspect of tragedy.

1. a once noble hero _____

_____

_____

_____

2. a terrible downfall _____

_____

_____

_____

3. a tragic flaw _____

_____

_____

_____

4. irreversible defeat or death _____

_____

_____

_____

5. wisdom or knowledge gained from suffering _____

_____

_____

_____

(Continued on page 92.)

ACT V

*Drama Study Guide: **The Tragedy of Othello, the Moor of Venice***

(Continued from page 91.)

Applying Skills

Some critics consider the character of Othello to be lacking several of the necessary qualities of a tragic hero. They point out, for instance, that Othello does not have as high a rank as Hamlet or King Lear and that his downfall is merely a personal one that affects no one beyond his immediate circle. Do you think Othello qualifies as a true tragic hero, or do you see reasons to deny him that status? Give specific examples from the play to support your opinion.

_____

_____

_____

_____

_____

Reader's Response

The character of Othello has been played by numerous actors, all of whom have brought their own special interpretation to the role. The African American actor Paul Robeson developed an Othello of quiet dignity and melancholy, whereas the British actor Laurence Olivier reinforced Othello's alien status and sensuous, proud nature. How would you play the character of Othello, especially in the final scene? Is his self-inflicted punishment an act of courage or pride? Is his obsession with the way others will speak of him an indication of an essentially narcissistic and self-dramatizing nature, or does it underscore the virtuous side of his personality, the part that yearns for truth and justice?

_____

_____

_____

_____

_____

_____

_____

_____

_____

*Drama Study Guide: **The Tragedy of Othello, the Moor of Venice***

Test, Act V

Thoughtful Reading *(40 points)*

On the line provided, write the letter of the *best* answer to each of the following items. *(8 points each)*

_____ **1.** In an aside in Scene 1, Iago tells the audience that

    a. he has grown fond of Roderigo
    b. he does not care whether Roderigo gets killed
    c. he wishes to spare Cassio's life
    d. Roderigo is too much of a coward to kill Cassio

_____ **2.** How does Othello react when he hears the wounded Cassio groaning?

    a. He is upset that Cassio is still alive.
    b. He becomes confused and doesn't know what to do next.
    c. He is sorry that his old friend Cassio is suffering.
    d. He is pleased and emboldened to act violently.

_____ **3.** Which of the following is *not* an example of Iago's hypocrisy?

    a. He instructs Emilia to keep silent.
    b. He uses his shirt to bind Cassio's wound.
    c. He kills Cassio's assailant.
    d. He is gracious to Lodovico and Gratiano.

_____ **4.** On whom does Iago try to cast blame for Roderigo's death?

    a. Cassio   **b.** Bianca   **c.** Othello   **d.** thieves

_____ **5.** Which of the following quotations expresses an important *theme* of the play?

    a. "Nay, guiltiness will speak, / Though tongues were out of use."
    b. "A guiltless death I die."
    c. "What should such a fool / Do with so good a wife?"
    d. "Then must you speak / Of one that loved not wisely but too well."

Expanded Response *(30 points)*

6. For which of the following characters in Act V do you have the most sympathy? On the lines provided, write the letter of the character you choose, describe the character's situation in Act V, and give reasons for your response. Use at least one example from the play to support your ideas. There is more than one possible answer. *(15 points)*

    a. Othello   **b.** Desdemona   **c.** Cassio   **d.** Emilia

_____

_____

_____

_____

_____

ACT V

(Continued on page 94.)

Drama Study Guide: The Tragedy of Othello, the Moor of Venice

(Continued from page 93.)

7. Match each of the quotations in the left-hand column below with its speaker. After each speaker's name in the right-hand column, write the letter of his or her quotation(s) and describe the speaker's emotional state when the words were spoken. Note that one speaker has two quotations. *(15 points)*

Quotation	Speaker's Emotional State
a. "He hath a daily beauty in his life / That makes me ugly."	Othello
b. "Kill me tomorrow; let me live tonight!"	Iago
c. "O gull! O dolt! / As ignorant as dirt!"	
d. "But why should honor outlive honesty? / Let it go all."	Desdemona
e. "From this time forth I never will speak word."	Emilia

Written Response *(30 points)*

8. Were you surprised by the death of Desdemona, Emilia, or Othello, or did it seem inevitable in light of what had already occurred? Choose one of these three characters, and on the lines below, write a paragraph describing the circumstances of his or her death and explaining whether or not you found the death surprising. Include at least two references to the play to support your view.

_____

_____

_____

_____

_____

_____

_____

_____

_____

_____

*Drama Study Guide: **The Tragedy of Othello, the Moor of Venice***

Making Meanings, the Play as a Whole

1. One of the major **themes** of *Othello* is the difficulty of distinguishing appearance from reality, or *seeming* from *being*. Which characters have such difficulties? What is Shakespeare saying about judgments based on appearances? Support your interpretation with examples from the text.

2. The fact that Othello is a career soldier has a profound effect on his character and his responses. Find examples in the play that show the influence of Othello's military background on his actions. Do you think this influence is enough to explain his behavior toward Desdemona? Why or why not?

3. How important do you think Othello's race is to the play? Could all references to his skin color be removed without essentially altering the play's meaning? Why or why not?

4. Early critics of *Othello* were disturbed by what they thought was an immoral ending: The innocent Desdemona is killed, and the evil Iago survives. What do you think of the ending of the play? Do audiences today demand moral endings to movies and to dramas on TV and stage? Discuss your responses to this question.

5. According to the critic G. R. Elliott, *Othello* is the world's supreme secular poem of human love. What do you think this means? Think of other poems, plays, and movies about great love, and decide if you would rank *Othello* among the best of them. Give reasons for your evaluation.

6. Some critics have argued that Othello lacks the nobility and the greatness of a true **tragic hero,** like Hamlet or King Lear, and that, as a result, his fall has less emotional impact on the audience. How do you think an audience today would view Othello? How would today's audience be affected by Othello's downfall?

Choices: Building Your Portfolio, the Play as a Whole

Creative Writing

1. Creating an Interior Monologue

Suppose that we could know Desdemona's thoughts as her husband murders her. What might she have said about her fate at the hands of the man she so loved and trusted? Write the thoughts of the dying Desdemona.

Critical Writing

2. A Victim of Deception

The critic Norman Sanders has written that "alone among the tragic heroes, Othello is a patient rather than an agent, worked on by forces outside himself, as total a victim of deception as any character in the Shakespearean canon." Decide whether you agree or disagree with this critical comment. Find evidence in the text to support your answer. Then, write a short essay in which you respond to Sanders.

Critical Writing

3. Shakespeare's Women

Two of the women in *Othello,* Desdemona and Emilia, are accused of betraying their husbands, although both are innocent. The third woman, Bianca, fears that her lover, Cassio, has been unfaithful to her. In an essay, discuss these women and what they might reveal about Shakespeare's attitude toward women. Consider how the three are alike and how they are different. Do you think Shakespeare had a broad or a narrow view of women's roles and personalities? Be sure to support your analysis with direct quotations.

Critical Writing

4. Analyzing the Character of Othello

Othello describes himself as a man not easily made jealous. What do you make of this statement? Is this an example of his lack of self-knowledge, or is there some truth to this description? Discuss your evaluation of Othello's character in a brief essay. In your analysis, make direct references to the text.

Critical Writing

5. Analyzing the Character of Iago

In the last scene in the play, Othello asks why Iago "hath thus ensnared my soul and body," but

Iago refuses to answer. Critics like Samuel Taylor Coleridge explain Iago's behavior as "motiveless malignity," or evil done for the sake of evil. How would you explain Iago? Do you think people like Iago exist in actual life? Write your assessment of Iago's character in a critical essay. Be sure to support your analysis with direct quotes from the play and with specific examples from everyday life.

Art/Dramatic Performance

6. Designing Costumes

Shakespeare's *Othello* has been set in different places and in different times, and its main character has appeared in a variety of styles, from a bewigged eighteenth-century British general to a turbaned sultan. In a small group, choose a time and place for this play about the marriage of an exotic foreigner and a local woman. When you have chosen your setting, draw costumes for Othello, Iago, and Desdemona that fit the location.

Research/Critical Thinking/ Speaking

7. Exploring Shakespeare's Sources

Othello is believed to be based partly on a sixteenth-century narrative titled *Hecatommithi* by the Italian writer Giraldi Cinthio. Research the similarities and differences between Shakespeare's *Othello* and Cinthio's tale of revenge, jealousy, and murder. Then, prepare an oral report, comparing and contrasting the play and this source. Speculate on why Shakespeare might have been inspired by Cinthio's narrative and why he changed some of the specific aspects of Cinthio's story. Also discuss what Shakespeare's version of the story achieves that Cinthio's does not.

Oral Interpretation

8. Performing a Scene

With a small group, choose a scene from *Othello,* and prepare a performance of it. First, choose a director, and have that person assign the roles. Then, with the director leading the discussion, let the actors explore the characters' thoughts, motives, and feelings. Also with the director, discuss the emotional impact the scene

(Continued on page 97.)

(Continued from page 96.)

is intended to deliver. Rehearse the scene until the director is satisfied that every actor's words, gestures, and movements get across the intended meaning and mood of the scene. Perform the scene with scenery, props, and costumes if possible.

Critical Writing

9. Responding to a Review

Othello is one of Shakespeare's most popular plays and has been staged and filmed numerous times. Try to see one of the film versions; either rent a video or check to see whether your school or public library has a copy. Then, do some research to locate a review of the version you have seen. In a short essay, compare that review with your own responses to the film. Do you agree with the reviewer's opinion, or do you think the reviewer must have seen a different movie?

Creative Writing

10. Staging *Othello*

Having read the Introduction to the HRW Classics edition of *Othello* (pages 1–20) and Alan Riding's article in that same book (pages 178–181), you will have a pretty good idea of what the original Globe Theater must have looked like and what it might have been like to be a member of the audience. Choose a scene in the play, and decide how it should be staged. Take into account the structure of the stage and the proximity of the audience. Or imagine that you are in the audience during a showing of *Othello* in 1604, and describe your experience.

Creative Writing

11. Writing a Prequel

Intense jealousy leads both Othello and the speaker in "The Laboratory" by Robert Browning (pages 172–174 of the HRW Classics edition of *Othello*) to commit heinous acts of murder. Each man kills the woman he loves most in order that she not belong to another. In the play we see how Iago works on Othello to incite his jealousy, but in "The Laboratory" we never hear the full story. Write a prequel—the opposite of a sequel—in which you describe what you think happened *before* the poem begins. Decide whether it is a single incident or a series of events that has pushed the speaker to commit the act of murder. Is the speaker being manipulated? Is he mentally unstable? Are there extenuating circumstances?

Drama Study Guide: The Tragedy of Othello, the Moor of Venice

Language Link Worksheet, the Play as a Whole

Shakespeare's Language

The language Shakespeare used is an early form of Modern English that is different from today's English in a variety of ways. The following list, with examples from *Othello,* describes some characteristics of Shakespeare's English. Whereas some of the following practices were observed in everyday speech, others were poetic conventions. Shakespeare often used contractions or omitted syllables in order to maintain the meter.

1. Shakespeare frequently made contractions of words that we write separately today. He also dropped letters, particularly vowels, at the ends of words and in the ending *-est.*

   > I gave her such a one; 'twas [it was] my first gift.
   > > —Act III, Scene 3, line 433

   > Be near at hand; I may miscarry in't [in it].
   > > —Act V, Scene 1, line 6

   > At this odd-even and dull watch o' th' [of the] night . . .
   > > —Act I, Scene 1, line 120

   > Thou cunning'st [cunningest] pattern of excelling nature . . .
   > > —Act V, Scene 2, line 11

2. Shakespeare omitted entire unstressed syllables from the beginning or middle of words.

   > I cannot 'twixt [betwixt] the heaven and the main
   >   Descry a sail.
   > > —Act II, Scene 1, lines 3–4

   > So sweet was ne'er [never] so fatal.
   > > —Act V, Scene 2, line 20

3. Shakespeare used many words (such as the adverbs *hence, thence, whence, hither, thither,* and *whither* and the pronouns *thy, thou, thee,* and *thine*) that we no longer or rarely use today. Words that have dropped out of the language are called *archaic.*

   > He went **hence** [from here] but now,
   > And certainly in strange unquietness.
   > > —Act III, Scene 4, lines 133–134

   > If I quench **thee** [you], **thou** [you] flaming minister,
   > I can again **thy** [your] former light restore. . . .
   > > —Act V, Scene 2, lines 8–9

4. Archaic words include forms of verbs with endings such as *-th* and *-st,* as well as irregular verb forms such as *spake* (spoke).

   > He **hath** [has] a daily beauty in his life. . . .
   > > —Act V, Scene 1, line 19

   > What **wouldst** [would] thou write of me, if thou **shouldst** [should] praise me?
   > > —Act II, Scene 1, line 116

   > She that I **spake** [spoke] of, our great captain's captain . . .
   > > —Act II, Scene 1, line 74

5. Shakespeare freely used words as different parts of speech, sometimes inventing words in the process.

   > But, good lieutenant, is your general **wived**? [The noun *wife* is used as a verb meaning "to have a wife."]
   > > —Act II, Scene 1, line 60

(Continued on page 99.)

*Drama Study Guide: **The Tragedy of Othello, the Moor of Venice***

(Continued from page 98.)

EXERCISE   **Understanding Shakespeare's Language**

Rewrite these lines from *Othello* in today's English, replacing the italicized, archaic words and spellings with more modern forms. You need not change the words in roman type.

1. . . . That *thou* Iago, who *hast* had my purse / As if the strings were *thine, shouldst* know of this. (Act I, Scene 1, lines 2–3)

_____

_____

2. Fathers, from *hence* trust not your daughters' minds. (Act I, Scene 1, line 167)

_____

_____

3. . . . Would ever have, *t'*incur a general *mock,* / Run from her guardage to the sooty bosom / Of such a thing as *thou* . . . (Act I, Scene 2, lines 68–70)

_____

_____

4. She swore, in faith, *'twas* strange, *'twas* passing strange. . . . (Act I, Scene 3, line 159)

_____

_____

5. *I prithee,* let *thy* wife *attend* on her. . . . (Act I, Scene 3, line 292)

_____

_____

6. *Methinks* the wind *hath* spoke aloud at land; / A fuller blast *ne'er* shook our battlements. / If it *hath ruffianed* so upon the sea, / What ribs of oak . . . / Can hold the mortise? (Act II, Scene 1, lines 5–9)

_____

_____

7. Come *hither.* If *thou be'st* valiant. . . . (Act II, Scene 1, lines 210–211)

_____

_____

(Continued on page 100.)

*Drama Study Guide: **The Tragedy of Othello, the Moor of Venice***

(Continued from page 99.)

8. *Didst thou* not see her paddle with the palm of his hand? (Act II, Scene 1, lines 250–251)

_____

_____

9. I think *thou dost;* / And, for all I know *thou'rt* full of love and honesty / And *weigh'st thy* words before *thou giv'st* them breath. . . . (Act III, Scene 3, lines 117–119)

_____

_____

10. *Fetch't,* let me *see't.* (Act III, Scene 4, line 86)

_____

_____

11. *Thou said'st*—O, it comes *o'er* my memory / As *doth* the raven *o'er* the infected house. . . . (Act IV, Scene 1, lines 20–21)

_____

_____

12. O *thou* weed, / Who *art* so lovely fair and *smell'st* so sweet . . . (Act IV, Scene 2, lines 66–67)

_____

_____

13. In *troth,* I think *thou wouldst* not. (Act IV, Scene 3, line 70)

_____

_____

14. Come, mistress, you must *tell's* another tale. . . . / And tell my lord and lady what *hath happed.* (Act V, Scene 1, lines 126–128)

_____

_____

15. *Ay,* and for that *thou diest.* (Act V, Scene 2, line 41)

_____

_____

*Drama Study Guide: **The Tragedy of Othello, the Moor of Venice***

100   HRW MATERIAL COPYRIGHTED UNDER NOTICE APPEARING EARLIER IN THIS WORK.

Test, the Play as a Whole

Responding to Literature *(100 points)*

1. Several characters in *Othello* tell lies, either routinely or at a critical moment when under the influence of a strong emotion. In the chart below, list three characters who lie in the play. Then, describe a lie each one tells, the emotion behind the lie, and one consequence of the lie. *(30 points)*

Character	Lie	Emotion	Consequence
1.			
2.			
3.			

2. The language of *Othello* is as poetic as the action is dramatic. In the second column of the chart below, write one specific example of the imagery named in the first column. Then, in the third column, briefly describe how each image contributes to the play's overall mood and theme. *(30 points)*

Imagery	Example	Effect on Mood and Theme
1. heaven and hell		
2. poison, disease, contamination		
3. love and death		

(Continued on page 102.)

*Drama Study Guide: **The Tragedy of Othello, the Moor of Venice***

(Continued from page 101.)

Respond to each question below. Use an extra sheet of paper if necessary. (*20 points each*)

3. Critic A. C. Bradley wrote, "The skill of Iago was extraordinary, but so was his good fortune." In what ways does fate or chance favor the fulfillment of Iago's schemes? Cite specific examples from the play, and then evaluate the relative roles of chance and choice in Othello's fall.

_____

_____

_____

_____

_____

_____

_____

_____

_____

4. When Othello, in Act V, Scene 2, enters Desdemona's bedroom to kill her, he says, "It is the cause, it is the cause, my soul." Re-read the scene and give your interpretation of Othello's words. Why does he think he must kill the woman he loves?

_____

_____

_____

_____

_____

_____

_____

_____

_____

_____

_____

*Drama Study Guide: **The Tragedy of Othello, the Moor of Venice***

Testing the Genre

Reading a Shakespearean Drama

Carefully read the following excerpt from Act III, Scene 4, of *The Tragedy of Hamlet, Prince of Denmark*. Then, answer the questions that follow.

Before the play starts, the king is murdered by his own brother, Claudius, who then assumes the crown and marries the queen. Sometime later Prince Hamlet is visited by his father's ghost, who asks Hamlet to avenge the murder. Hamlet, convinced that he must kill Claudius, begins to behave erratically. In this scene, Polonius, advisor to the new king, has asked Queen Gertrude, Hamlet's mother, to demand better behavior of Hamlet. As Hamlet approaches, Polonius hides behind an arras (a drape) to observe Hamlet's responses.

FROM *The Tragedy of Hamlet, Prince of Denmark* by William Shakespeare

The Queen's closet. Enter Hamlet.

Hamlet.	Now, mother, what's the matter?	
Queen.	Hamlet, thou hast thy father much offended.	
Hamlet.	Mother, you have my father much offended.	
Queen.	Come, come, you answer with an idle tongue.	
Hamlet.	Go, go, you question with a wicked tongue.	5
Queen.	Why, how now, Hamlet!	
Hamlet.	What's the matter now?	
Queen.	Have you forgot me?	
Hamlet.	No, by the rood, not so!	
	You are the Queen, your husband's brother's wife.	
	And—would it were not so—you are my mother.	
Queen.	Nay, then, I'll set those to you that can speak.	10
Hamlet.	Come, come, and sit you down, you shall not budge!	
	You go not till I set you up a glass	
	Where you may see the inmost part of you.	
Queen.	What wilt thou do? Thou wilt not murder me?	
	Help, help, ho!	15
Polonius.	[*Behind.*] What, ho! help, help, help!	
Hamlet.	[*Draws.*] How now! a rat? Dead for a ducat, dead!	

Makes a pass through the arras and kills Polonius.

Polonius.	[*Behind.*]	
	O, I am slain!	
Queen.	O me, what hast thou done.	
Hamlet.	Nay, I know not. Is it the King?	
Queen.	O, what a rash and bloody deed is this!	20
Hamlet.	A bloody deed—almost as bad, good mother,	
	As kill a king, and marry with his brother	
Queen.	As kill a king?	
Hamlet.	Ay, lady, 'twas my word.	

Lifts up the arras and discovers Polonius.

	Thou wretched, rash, intruding fool, farewell!	
	I took thee for thy better. Take thy fortune.	25
	Thou find'st to be too busy is some danger—	
	Leave wringing of your hands. Peace! sit you down	
	And let me wring your heart; for so I shall	
	If it be made of penetrable stuff;	

(Continued on page 104.)

Drama Study Guide: The Tragedy of Othello, the Moor of Venice

(Continued from page 103.)

If damned custom have not brazed it so   30
That it is proof and bulwark against sense.

Queen. What have I done, that thou dar'st wag thy tongue
In noise so rude against me?

Hamlet.   Such an act
That blurs the grace and blush of modesty;
Calls virtue hypocrite; takes off the rose   35
From the fair forehead of an innocent love,
And sets a blister there; makes marriage vows
As false as dicers' oaths. O, such a deed
As from the body of contraction[1] plucks
The very soul, and sweet religion makes   40
A rhapsody of words![2] Heaven's face doth glow;
Yea, this solidity and compound mass,[3]
With tristful visage, as against the doom,[4]
Is thought-sick at the act.

Queen.   Ay me, what act,
That roars so loud, and thunders in the index?[5]   45

Hamlet. Look here, upon this picture, and on this,
The counterfeit presentment of two brothers.
See what a grace was seated on this brow;
Hyperion's curls; the front of Jove himself;
An eye like Mars, to threaten and command;   50
A station[6] like the herald Mercury
New lighted on a heaven-kissing hill:
A combination and a form indeed
Where every god did seem to set his seal
To give the world assurance of a man.   55
This was your husband. Look you now what follows.
Here is your husband, like a mildewed ear
Blasting his wholesome brother. Have you eyes?
Could you on this fair mountain leave to feed
And batten[7] on this moor? Ha! have you eyes?   60
You cannot call it love; for at your age
The heyday in the blood is tame; it's humble,
And waits upon the judgment; and what judgment
Would step from this to this? Sense sure you have,
Else could you not have motion; but sure that sense   65
Is apoplexed;[8] for madness would not err,
Nor sense to ecstasy was ne'er so thralled
But it reserved some quantity of choice
To serve in such a difference.[9] What devil was't

---

1. **contraction:** marriage contract.
2. **rhapsody of words:** string of meaningless words.
3. **solidity ... mass:** solid earth.
4. **tristful ... doom:** mournful face, as if waiting for Doomsday.
5. **what act ... index:** if the beginning (index, or list of contents) is so troublesome, what will follow?
6. **station:** figure; physique.
7. **batten:** gorge; fatten.
8. **apoplexed:** paralyzed.
9. **serve ... difference:** enable you to see the difference between your former husband and your present one.

(Continued on page 105.)

*Drama Study Guide: **The Tragedy of Othello, the Moor of Venice***

(Continued from page 104.)

That thus hath cozened[10] you at hoodman-blind?[11]   70
Eyes without feeling, feeling without sight,
Ears without hands or eyes, smelling sans[12] all,
Or but a sickly part of one true sense
Could not so mope.[13] . . .

Queen.   O Hamlet, speak no more!
Thou turn'st mine eyes into my very soul,   75
And there I see such black and grained spots
As will not leave their tinct.

Hamlet.   Nay, but to live
In the rank sweat of an enseamed[14] bed,
Stewed in corruption, honeying and making love
Over the nasty sty!

Queen.   O, speak to me no more!   80
These words, like daggers, enter in mine ears.
No more, sweet Hamlet!

Hamlet.   A murderer and a villain!
A slave that is not twentieth part the tithe
Of your precedent[15] lord; a vice of kings;[16]
A cutpurse of the empire and the rule,   85
That from a shelf the precious diadem stole
And put it in his pocket!

Queen.   No more!

---

10. **cozened:** tricked, cheated.
11. **hoodman-blind:** blindman's buff.
12. **sans:** without.
13. **mope:** be dull.

14. **enseamed:** soiled; greasy.
15. **precedent:** former.
16. **vice of kings:** caricature of a king.

Understanding Vocabulary *(20 points)*

Each underlined word below has also been underlined in the excerpt from *Hamlet*. Re-read those passages, and use context clues to help you select an answer. Write the letter of the word(s) that *best* complete(s) each sentence. *(4 points each)*

_____ **1.** A rash act is one that is
      a. reasonable   **b.** generous   **c.** reckless   **d.** wise

_____ **2.** To wring the heart is to
      a. torment it   **b.** encourage it   **c.** desire it   **d.** request it

_____ **3.** A bulwark provides
      a. encouragement   **b.** a barrier   **c.** information   **d.** an entrance

_____ **4.** An object that is mildewed is
      a. old and cracked   **b.** withered   **c.** peeling   **d.** damp and moldy

_____ **5.** Corruption is a state of
      a. moral decay   **b.** uncertainty   **c.** anxiety   **d.** hopeful anticipation

(Continued on page 106.)

Drama Study Guide: The Tragedy of Othello, the Moor of Venice

(Continued from page 105.)

Thoughtful Reading *(35 points)*

On the line provided, write the letter of the *best* answer to each of the following items. *(7 points each)*

_____ **6.** Which words best describe the tone Hamlet takes with his mother before he is distracted by Polonius's shouts?

    a. playful and vague   **c.** sad and serious
    b. slyly accusing   **d.** loving and forgiving

_____ **7.** What causes Polonius to cry out from his hiding place?

    a. As planned, he is calling the palace guard to arrest Hamlet.
    b. He has had a fainting spell and wants Hamlet to help him.
    c. He is afraid Hamlet will storm out without listening to what his mother has to say.
    d. He believes Hamlet is about to assault his mother.

_____ **8.** When Hamlet discovers the body of Polonius, he says, "I took thee for thy better," referring to

    a. the ghost of Hamlet's father   **c.** King Claudius
    b. his friend Horatio   **d.** Gertrude

_____ **9.** What physical objects does Hamlet use to illustrate his argument with his mother?

    a. pictures of the present and past kings
    b. two mirrors, one of which is cracked
    c. statues of Jove and Mercury
    d. pictures of a mountain and a moor

_____ **10.** Hamlet's language when speaking of his mother's relationship with Claudius contains images of

    a. sorcery   **c.** excess and decay
    b. love and devotion   **d.** torture and punishment

Expanded Response *(15 points)*

11. Which of the following statements do you think *best* explains Hamlet's purpose for going to his mother's room? On a separate sheet of paper, write the letter of the answer you choose and briefly defend your choice. There is more than one possible answer. Use at least one example from the excerpt to support your ideas.

    a. Hamlet hates his mother and wants to break all ties with her.
    b. He wants his mother to feel ashamed of her marriage to Claudius.
    c. He wishes to hurt his mother because she has hurt him.
    d. He wants his mother to turn her attention away from Claudius and toward him instead.

Written Response *(30 points)*

12. Hamlet, like Othello, accuses a woman close to him of treachery. Of course, Hamlet is accusing his mother and Othello, his wife, yet there are similarities (as well as differences) in their actions, motives, and emotions. On a separate sheet of paper, write a paragraph that compares and contrasts Hamlet's treatment of his mother and Othello's treatment of Desdemona. Support your ideas with at least two specific references to *Othello* and to the excerpt from *Hamlet*.

Drama Study Guide: ***The Tragedy of Othello, the Moor of Venice***

Cross-Curricular Activity

Social Studies

Assignment

As a military man fighting for a foreign state, Othello is part of a long-standing military tradition practiced in the city-state of Venice and elsewhere: the use of mercenaries. Most soldiers fight for their own country, either as volunteers or as draftees. Mercenary soldiers, on the other hand, fight for hire in a foreign army. Although nowadays *mercenary* often refers to someone motivated by greed, throughout history mercenaries have been professionals who have prided themselves on their skill in waging war.

For this assignment you will work alone or with a partner to research mercenaries in sixteenth-century Venice or another setting in which mercenaries played a significant role. You will then compose a letter that a mercenary in that setting might have written to someone back home. In the letter you will try to present a vivid picture of what military life was like for the writer and describe how he felt about the country that hired him. Afterward you will read your letter aloud to the class and state your views on the use of mercenaries in the setting you chose.

Materials

- Index cards

Selecting a Place and Time and Planning Your Letter

You may begin your research by reading about mercenaries in an encyclopedia. Find out about conflicts in which mercenaries played an important role. (The American Revolution and wars in twentieth-century Africa are good examples.) Then, choose a country that has employed mercenaries and look in an on-line or card catalog for sources on its military history. Biographies, memoirs, letters, and interviews may be good sources of information about a mercenary's experiences.

Next, make a list of questions, such as the following, to be answered in your letter:

- Is your mercenary an officer or a member of the rank and file?
- What is his country of origin? How does he feel about being away from it?
- For whom is he fighting? Who is the enemy?
- What are his military duties? How well is he paid?
- What are his living conditions like?
- How does he feel about those who employ him? How do they feel about him?

Preparing Your Letter

On index cards, take notes on information that answers your research questions. Record the title, author, publisher, date of publication, and page number(s) of your sources in case you have to go back to check facts or find additional information. Then, read your notes and select details to include in your letter. As you look over the information you have gathered, try to form an opinion about mercenary life in the period you have researched.

You may want to use the following three-paragraph structure for your letter:

1. Introduce the setting and the writer.
2. Give details of military life.
3. Describe how the writer feels about fighting as a mercenary in the conflict you describe.

Sharing What You Have Learned

Read your letter to your class or to a group, and discuss the advantages and disadvantages of using mercenaries in the setting you chose. After the other students have read their letters, compare and contrast the experiences described, and try to draw some conclusions about the use of mercenaries both in the past and in the present. Then, explore this question: Should nations continue hiring mercenaries to fight their wars?

Peer/Self-Evaluation

In evaluating your written and oral work for this assignment, consider these points:

- Did your letter provide an accurate and detailed picture of life for a mercenary in the setting you chose?
- Now that you've heard other students' letters, what would you change in your own letter?
- How did the information in other students' letters influence your ideas about the life of a mercenary?

Read On

"The Cask of Amontillado" and "Hop-Frog" by Edgar Allan Poe

Perhaps to get even with a world that he felt had rejected him, Edgar Allan Poe became a master at writing stories of revenge. In "The Cask of Amontillado" the aristocratic Montresor goes to great lengths—and subterranean depths—to avenge the *un*fortunate Fortunato. In "Hop-Frog" two dwarfs finally exact a terrible vengeance for inhumane treatment at the hands of their king and master.

Wuthering Heights by Emily Brontë

Wuthering is an Old English term for "turbulent weather." Turbulent Heights would be a good nickname for the mansion whose name is the title of Emily Brontë's *Wuthering Heights*. Hard rains, thundering skies, and bolts of lightning provide a suitable backdrop for a haunting, mystical tale of love and revenge. The bond between Brontë's hero and heroine, Heathcliff and Catherine, is stronger than life itself—but will love or vengeance win out in the end?

"My Last Duchess" by Robert Browning

The duke who narrates Browning's poem "My Last Duchess" had grown insanely jealous of his wife, the duchess. Her generosity and kindness, as seen through the duke's eyes, were coquetry and deception. With slowly dawning horror, the reader discovers the gruesome act that the duke's passions have led him to commit.

Le Morte Darthur (The Death of Arthur) by Sir Thomas Malory

Written by Sir Thomas Malory while in prison, *Le Morte Darthur* is a splendid retelling of the legendary tales of King Arthur. Chivalrous knights, exciting tournaments, and heroic quests are the stuff of legend. Malory breathes life into these tales, including the legend of Sir Lancelot and Queen Guinevere, whose betrayal of King Arthur brings about the destruction of Camelot.

Answer Key

Graphic Organizer for Active Reading, Act I

Graphic Organizer

Responses will vary. Sample responses follow.

Othello-Iago—The relationship is apparently based on trust, mutual need, and affection.

Othello-Desdemona—The relationship is apparently based on love, trust, and respect.

Iago-Roderigo—The relationship is apparently based on friendship, trust, and mutual need.

1. Since students are limited to the facts presented in Act I, they will probably choose Othello and Iago. They should cite Iago's words to show that he really hates Othello, is only pretending to be his devoted servant, and is really planning to get revenge on him. They should cite Othello's words to show that he likes, trusts, and depends on Iago.

2. Students may predict that Othello and Iago's relationship will change when Othello learns of Iago's treachery; that Othello and Desdemona's relationship will change when Iago puts his plan into action; or that Iago and Roderigo's relationship will change when Roderigo realizes that he is being used by Iago.

Making Meanings, Act I

Reviewing the Text

a. Iago is angry because Othello has chosen Cassio, not him, as his second in command despite Iago's belief in his own superior record and ability.

b. Although Iago now hates Othello, he plans to be outwardly loyal to the general while secretly plotting to get revenge.

c. Brabantio is upset because his daughter married without his consent and because he finds repulsive and unnatural her union with a black man.

d. Desdemona states that although she respects her father, she has willingly pledged her loyalty to Othello, as her mother pledged hers to her husband.

e. Othello judges Iago to be loyal, honest, and trustworthy. His placing Desdemona in Iago's care (while she prepares to follow her husband to Cyprus) reflects this judgment.

First Thoughts

1. Responses will vary. Sample response: Othello is an experienced, disciplined soldier and leader who seems confident of his own ability and appears to have the confidence of his superiors. At this point in the play, most students will probably be willing to entrust their country's safety to him.

Shaping Interpretations

2. Roderigo is hostile toward Othello because he, Roderigo, wanted to marry Desdemona but was rejected by her and her father; now the Moor is enjoying what Roderigo believes he desires. Brabantio is hostile toward Othello because he cannot accept that his daughter willingly married this man of another race and so suspects him of casting a spell to make her love him. Iago's hostility is colder, less open, and less impulsive than that of Roderigo and Brabantio. Iago calculates patiently, whereas the others complain and act ineffectively.

3. Othello responds calmly and confidently in both cases. He does not become defensive in the face of Brabantio's insulting accusations and coolly breaks up the mock fight between Roderigo and Iago. These actions reveal that he trusts Desdemona will stand by him loyally and seems to know his worth to the state.

4. Othello characterizes himself as a veteran soldier, unsophisticated in the ways of civilian life and simple in his speech. Students may notice that although he does have many qualities associated with the military man, his words to the senators, contrary to his suggestion, are effective, even poetic.

5. Responses will vary. Some students may truly believe that people should be judged by appearances, but most will disagree. Those students should note that Iago is the perfect example of someone whose appearance of honesty is deceptive.

6. The duke and the senators respect Othello as a military leader. Iago privately says, "The Moor is of a free and open nature / That thinks men honest that but seem to be so" (Scene 3, lines 391–392) and suggests that he can therefore be easily misled.

7. Othello tells the senators that as a guest in Brabantio's home he related stories, at Brabantio's request, of his boyhood experi-

ences and his military adventures in far-flung parts of the world, and these tales moved Desdemona to love him. When asking for permission to accompany Othello to Cyprus, Desdemona says that "to his honors and his valiant parts / Did I my soul and fortunes consecrate" (Scene 3, lines 249–250), suggesting that her love is so great that she would rather be at Othello's side at war than at home alone.

8. Roderigo appears to be foolish, sensual, and petulant, ready to give up when he cannot get what he wants—Desdemona. Iago is shown to be cynical (seeing as lust what Roderigo calls love) and too coldly self-centered to ever consider killing himself because he has not won the love of another human being. Hate comes easier than love to Iago, and unlike his dupe, Roderigo, he is patient and cunning in pursuing what he wants.

9. Though Iago doesn't know whether the rumor is true, he reveals that people have said that Othello is in love with Iago's wife. His plan is to get Cassio's position and get even with Othello by slyly suggesting to him that Cassio loves Desdemona.

Challenging the Text

10. Responses will vary. Sample response: Because Desdemona is young and has lived a sheltered life, the adventurous, older, worldly Othello, with his tales of dangerous encounters in foreign lands, stimulates her imagination. She is no doubt attracted by his courage and perhaps intrigued by his exotic background. Most students will find their love believable in the context of the play.

Words to Own Worksheet, Act I

Developing Vocabulary

Sentences will vary. Sample responses follow. Vocabulary words are shown in italics.

1. Michael claimed that his remark was not *obsequious* but a genuine compliment.

2. Her parents had set an early curfew, and this was a *vexation* for Keisha.

3. A *timorous* attitude is definitely not an advantage for athletes.

4. The coach demanded that his players show *civility* to one another.

5. The old man vowed that the *iniquity* he had suffered would not go unpunished.

6. Tom made his *grievance* publicly known, and his neighbors were sympathetic.

7. They will *promulgate* the minimum-speed-limit law by hiring additional police.

8. The lump on his skull was barely *palpable* now that two weeks had elapsed since the fight.

9. She accomplished the task in a *facile* manner, even though it was extremely difficult.

10. In the 1950s, many people believed that nuclear war was *imminent*.

Literary Elements Worksheet, Act I

Understanding Irony

1. verbal; The discrepancy is between Roderigo's seemingly respectful and innocent words and his vengeful intention.

2. verbal; The discrepancy is between Iago's stated reluctance to do harm and his actual relish of destruction.

3. dramatic; The discrepancy is between what the duke does not know and what the audience does know—that the beguiler of Desdemona is the state's military hero, Othello.

4. verbal; The discrepancy is between Othello's claim to lack oratorical skill and the actual effectiveness of his speech.

5. situational; The contrast is between the characterization of Desdemona as a shy, fearful, obedient young woman and the fact that she has boldly eloped with Othello.

6. situational; The contrast is between Iago's appearance as an honest, trustworthy man and the fact that Iago is Othello's enemy and the last person to whom Othello should be entrusting his wife's safety.

Applying Skills

Responses will vary. It will be obvious to most students that Iago, who has no difficulty distinguishing reality from unreality, is manipulating appearances. In this act, Brabantio, Roderigo, and Othello have difficulty distinguishing between appearances and reality. Roderigo, believing that Iago is helping him, is blind to the fact that he is being manipulated. Brabantio trusts Roderigo and Iago rather than Othello, the person who actually has Brabantio's daughter's welfare in mind. Othello places his trust in "honest Iago," who in fact is planning to destroy him.

Reader's Response

Responses will vary. Most students will agree that distinguishing appearance from reality is an important real-life skill to master. They might mention various social situations or commercial transactions (buying a used bicycle, for example) in which it is important to interpret successfully a person's character, intentions, or motives.

Test, Act I

Thoughtful Reading

1. a   **2.** d   **3.** c   **4.** a   **5.** d

Expanded Response

6. Responses will vary. Students should mention at least one conflict from the play to support their ideas.

   a. The speaker is Iago. Students may mention that this is the first reference the play makes to Iago's jealousy of Cassio and his resentment of Othello. Othello's choice of Cassio as his lieutenant becomes the motivating force for Iago's cruelty and deception throughout the play.

   b. The speaker is Brabantio. Students may mention the conflict between Brabantio and Othello or the conflict between Brabantio and Desdemona. At this point, Brabantio is placing all the blame on Othello, referring to Desdemona as "corrupted." Othello's corruption of her is Brabantio's explanation for her actions.

   c. The speaker is Desdemona. Students may point to Desdemona's conflict with her father over her elopement. A better response, however, might point to Desdemona's inner conflict. She loves both her new husband and her father and feels she cannot please them both.

   d. The speaker is Roderigo, and he is addressing Iago. Students should mention Roderigo's inner conflict. He is distraught because Desdemona, the woman he loves, has married Othello. He is hopeless and ready to end his life rather than angry and ready to exact revenge (which is what Iago is planning to do).

7. Responses will vary. Students should supply at least one line of dialogue spoken by Othello, an example of at least one action taken by Othello, and at least one line of dialogue spoken by another character about Othello. For each of these, students should supply a corresponding character trait. Sample responses follow.

   Othello's Words—"by your gracious patience, / I will a round unvarnished tale deliver / Of my whole course of love—what drugs, what charms, / What conjuration, and what mighty magic, / For such proceeding I am charged withal, / I won his daughter—" (Act I, Scene 3, lines 89–95). *Character Trait Revealed*—He is sincere and honest.

   Othello's Actions—He confides in Iago about his love for Desdemona (Act I, Scene 3, lines 290–296). *Character Trait Revealed*—He is too trusting.

   Others' Words About Othello—Iago: "Another of his fathom they have none / To lead their business" (Act I, Scene 1, lines 149–150). *Character Trait Revealed*—Othello is an excellent soldier.

Written Response

8. Responses will vary. In a model response, students should fulfill the following criteria:

   • demonstrate understanding of the prompt

   • clearly describe how Shakespeare creates the sense that Desdemona and Othello's happy marriage is in danger

   • support their ideas with at least two references to specific details in the play. For example:

      • Iago plants in Roderigo's head the idea that he may still be able to win Desdemona's heart.

      • The impending war in Cyprus threatens to interrupt the newlyweds' bliss.

Graphic Organizer for Active Reading, Act II

Graphic Organizer

Responses will vary. Sample responses follow.

Brabantio—Act I, Scene 2, lines 76–78: "I therefore apprehend and do attach thee / For an abuser of the world, a practicer / Of arts inhibited and out of warrant."

Iago—Act I, Scene 3, lines 391–394: "The Moor is of a free and open nature / That thinks men honest that but seem to be so; / And will as tenderly be led by th' nose / As asses are."

Desdemona—Act I, Scene 3, lines 248–250: "I saw Othello's visage in his mind, / And to his honors and his valiant parts / Did I my soul and fortunes consecrate."

Drama Study Guide: The Tragedy of Othello, the Moor of Venice

HRW MATERIAL COPYRIGHTED UNDER NOTICE APPEARING EARLIER IN THIS WORK.

111

1. Students will probably say that these lines reveal that Othello puts duty before friendship or that he has allowed his temper to get the best of him.

2. Answers will vary. Students may say that Othello's action in dismissing Cassio supports Iago's claim that Othello is easily led, or they may say that Othello's honorable love for Desdemona and hers for him contradict Brabantio's claim that Othello has used witchcraft or tricks to win Desdemona.

Making Meanings, Act II

Reviewing the Text

a. Cassio arrives first, followed by Desdemona, Emilia, Iago, and Roderigo. Othello arrives last.

b. When the Turkish fleet is destroyed in a storm at sea, the threat dissipates.

c. Iago incites Roderigo to fight with Cassio, who has had too much to drink.

d. Othello gets angry and strips Cassio of the rank of lieutenant and dismisses him as his second in command.

e. Iago advises Cassio to seek Desdemona's help in persuading Othello to reinstate him.

First Thoughts

1. Responses will vary. Most students will be attracted by the great love and passion that Othello and Desdemona express for each other and will wish them happiness. Iago is repelled by their love, jealous of Othello, and further persuaded to wreck Othello's happiness.

Shaping Interpretations

2. The setting moves from the city of Venice to a fortified seaport on the island of Cyprus. On a symbolic level the action moves from a highly civilized and orderly city-state to a less civilized and less secure outpost. Here, violence has occurred and seems likely to break out again at any moment if the Venetian authorities do not maintain control.

3. Cassio speaks of Desdemona with great respect and high praise. The fact that he greets Emilia boldly and informally, kissing her on the mouth, suggests that he is a flirt who expects women to welcome his attentions.

4. Iago views women cynically and hostilely. He uses clever language, including puns and paradoxes, to express his cold and mean-spirited evaluations. Cassio uses high-minded exaggerations to speak of Desdemona's beauty and virtues.

5. Although Othello is very happy, he speaks immediately of disasters and death—"If it were now to die, / 'Twere now to be most happy" (Scene 1, lines 185–186)—and expresses fears about what can follow such complete happiness.

6. Iago arouses Roderigo's jealousy of Cassio by convincing him that Desdemona has tired of Othello and is now in love with Cassio. After Cassio admits that he cannot tolerate alcohol, Iago talks Cassio into drinking too much so that he readily loses his temper when provoked by Roderigo. These actions reveal Iago to be a shrewd judge of others' weaknesses and an unscrupulous manipulator who will use others to achieve his own vengeful ends.

7. Lines from Scene 3 with imagery of hell, darkness, disease, and traps include these: "Divinity of hell! / When devils will the blackest sins put on, / They do suggest at first with heavenly shows / As I do now" (lines 341–344); "I'll pour this pestilence into his ear" (line 347); and "So will I turn her virtue into pitch, / And out of her own goodness make the net / That shall enmesh them all" (lines 351–353).

Extending the Text

8. Responses will vary. Some students may point to people who, like Iago, have been motivated by jealousy, hatred, or pride to commit crimes. Others may see Iago as more consistently evil and more relentlessly calculating than any real-life human being could ever be.

Challenging the Text

9. Responses will vary. In the reunion scene, Othello does question whether his new-found happiness can continue—"[This content] stops me here; it is too much of joy" (Scene 1, line 193) can be read as outright discomfort with happiness itself.

Words to Own Worksheet, Act II

Developing Vocabulary

Sentences will vary. Sample responses follow. Vocabulary words are shown in italics.

1. They *discern* a certain discomfort in their guest even though they are trying to make him feel at home.

Drama Study Guide: The Tragedy of Othello, the Moor of Venice

2. The *citadel* that overlooked the old city no longer served its original purpose; it was now a tourist attraction.

3. Even though he was upset, he tried to be *discreet* when he talked to the reporters, because he didn't want the news to reach the public.

4. The imminent arrival of the *eminent* scholar caused quite a stir on the college campus.

5. Lack of money is an *impediment* for many when they want to travel.

6. The poet's metaphor compared the process of erosion to eating; she imagined that the winds *gnaw* constantly at the earth's surface.

7. Whenever I take my sister's CDs without asking, a lecture is sure to *ensue.*

8. *Barbarous* treatment of minorities is a sad fact in many countries, including our own.

9. The *censure* of many of its readers caused the newspaper to censor itself.

10. Since this was not a special occasion, they seemed to be celebrating with *inordinate* enthusiasm.

Literary Elements Worksheet, Act II

Understanding Imagery

1. hunting or trapping; Iago is predatory and takes delight in doing harm. The sentence that extends this pattern is Scene 1, lines 167–168 ("I will gyve thee in thine own courtship").

2. eating and the supernatural; Desdemona; Othello.

3. poison or disease; Thought and poison are directly compared. Iago claims that revenge is what he feeds upon; it is his "diet" (Scene 2, line 290).

4. an animal—specifically, a dog; Cassio; Yes, Cassio becomes quarrelsome when drunk.

5. the supernatural; wine and the devil; "Every inordinate cup is unblest, and the ingredient is a devil" (Scene 3, lines 300–301).

6. disease or poison; He sees himself as having the power to corrupt and destroy others. It creates an ominous, evil atmosphere.

7. trapping; Desdemona; Scene 1, lines 166–167.

Applying Skills

Responses will vary.

Test, Act II
Thoughtful Reading

1. c   2. a   3. b   4. c   5. a

Expanded Response

6. Responses will vary. Students should mention at least one character trait for each speaker and link that trait to the line that is quoted. Sample responses follow.

   a. The speaker is Iago. Responses should address the key word in this line, *critical.* For Iago the word has multiple meanings. It means he is discerning; he is clever and analytical; he has little praise for others but sees only their faults; and finally, he is important in that he will decide the fates of all the play's major characters.

   b. The speaker is Desdemona. Responses might address the fact that for the first time Desdemona appears to be representing herself falsely. She is pretending to be "merry" even though she is not—in order, perhaps, to convince herself or those around her that she is not anxious about Othello or about Iago's mistreatment of her. Desdemona's white lies, of course, will enable Iago to carry out his schemes later in the play.

   c. The speaker is Othello. Responses might focus on Othello's love for Desdemona. We know him to be a character who says what he means, and his joy here is sincere.

   d. The speaker is Cassio. Students might note a few important elements of Cassio's character here. He is concerned about his "reputation"—what others think of him. He is also concerned with ethical behavior and thinks that he has betrayed "the immortal part" of himself. He considers his actions "bestial," beneath him. It is also important that he, like Othello, still trusts Iago enough to confide in him, giving Iago the ammunition he needs to fulfill his schemes.

7. Responses will vary. Students must list at least one character for each emotion listed below and then supply one action motivated by that emotion. Sample responses:

   Emotion—anger; *Character*—Cassio; *Action*—engages Roderigo in a brawl.

   Emotion—love; *Character*—Othello; *Action*—spends his time with Desdemona rather than overseeing the celebration.

   Emotion—envy; *Character*—Iago; *Action*—takes advantage of Cassio's drunkenness to make him look bad.

HRW MATERIAL COPYRIGHTED UNDER NOTICE APPEARING EARLIER IN THIS WORK.

113

ANSWER KEY

Written Response

8. Responses will vary. In a model response students should fulfill the following criteria:
   - demonstrate understanding of the prompt
   - clearly describe Iago's strategy—step by step—for destroying Othello
   - support their ideas with at least two references to specific details—preferably from Iago's soliloquies—in the play. For example:
     - In the soliloquy that ends Act I, Iago professes his hatred for Othello and his determination to get Cassio's position—that of lieutenant—for himself.
     - After instigating the brawl between Cassio and Roderigo, Iago persuades Cassio to plead with Desdemona to speak to Othello on his (Cassio's) behalf; all the while, Iago is planning to convince Othello that Cassio is in love with Desdemona.

Graphic Organizer for Active Reading, Act III

Graphic Organizer

Responses will vary. A sample response follows.

Iago's Evidence—Cassio and Desdemona are together, and Cassio "steals away" when Othello arrives; Desdemona deceived her father (and therefore, Iago implies, might also deceive Othello); Iago heard Cassio speak of Desdemona in his sleep; Iago has seen Cassio with the handkerchief that Othello gave Desdemona.

Evaluation of the Evidence—Students should recognize each instance of Iago's deceit. Only the suggestion that Desdemona is capable of deceiving Othello cannot be denied.

1. Answers will depend on students' evaluation of the evidence. Most students will probably say that Iago has not proved his case.

2. Answers will vary. Some students might begin to see that Othello's insecurities account for his behavior. He is older than his wife, their courtship was very short, and he may be wondering whether she can love someone as different from her as he is. Students may also remember Iago's claim that Othello is very gullible and may say that this trait helps account for his behavior.

Making Meanings, Act III

Reviewing the Text

a. She repeatedly urges Othello to forgive Cassio and restore him to his position as lieutenant.

b. Iago calls attention to Cassio's quickly leaving Desdemona as Othello approaches, slyly suggesting that there is something "guilty-like" in Cassio's movements (line 39).

c. Desdemona inadvertently drops the handkerchief. Emilia picks it up and gives it to Iago, who plants it in Cassio's room. Cassio then gives it to Bianca.

d. Othello demands that Iago give him "ocular [visible] proof" of Desdemona's infidelity.

e. Iago lies to Othello about the handkerchief and about Cassio's dream. Desdemona lies to Othello about losing the handkerchief. Emilia lies when Desdemona asks her whether she has seen the handkerchief.

First Thoughts

1. Responses will vary. Some students will feel pity as Othello is so masterfully manipulated by the evil Iago. Others will be disappointed in his lack of faith in the woman he loves and in his inability to see through Iago's lies and misrepresentations.

Shaping Interpretations

2. In order to make himself more credible, Iago deliberately gives the impression that he is reluctant to speak ill of Cassio. At the same time, he drops hints that inflame Othello's imagination and lead him to demand that Iago share his suspicions. While Iago is counseling Othello not to jump to conclusions, he is also advising him to watch Desdemona carefully to see whether she betrays any signs of guilt, thus setting Othello up to misread what he sees.

3. Iago warns Othello against jealousy, "the green-eyed monster which doth mock / The meat it feeds on" (Scene 3, lines 166–167). His warning is a bold example of dramatic irony, for the audience knows that his true intention is to arouse in Othello the very emotion he is warning him against.

4. In Scene 3, Othello expresses doubt and trust when he says of Desdemona "I think my wife be honest, and think she is not" (line 381). The contradictory emotions of love and hatred are revealed in Othello's use of contrasting images of heaven and hell and light and dark, such as the following: "Her name, that was as fresh / As Dian's visage, is now begrimed and black / As mine own face" (lines 383–385), and "the fair devil" (line 475).

5. By the end of Scene 3, Othello has decided to trust Iago above everyone else, and he orders Iago, whom he calls his lieutenant, to kill

*Drama Study Guide: **The Tragedy of Othello, the Moor of Venice***

Cassio. Othello has forsaken Desdemona, Cassio, and all they stand for and has allied himself completely with Iago.

6. Bianca, Cassio's mistress, becomes jealous when he gives her a handkerchief she knows belongs to another woman. Roderigo is jealous of Othello and becomes jealous of Cassio as well when Iago convinces him that Desdemona has taken Cassio as a lover. Iago himself is envious of Othello and Cassio for a variety of reasons, including professional jealousy and a kind of general envy of the good character and reputation of each.

7. Our imaginations are very powerful and affect how we perceive the world; such feelings as jealousy can alter our judgment, making us interpret events or people's behavior in a negtive way.

8. Images of consumption have run through the play. This metaphor is fitting because a jealous person is tormented by thoughts and feelings; that is, he or she is "consumed" by suspicions. And so jealousy is envisioned as a creature with a monstrous appetite.

Extending the Text

9. Responses will vary. Images of jealousy might include a weapon, a spice, a cage, a crutch, or a toy.

Challenging the Text

10. Responses will vary. Most students will agree that Shakespeare provides some plausible motives for Othello's jealousy—his insecurity about his age and appearance, the brevity of his marriage, and his belief in Iago's honesty. In addition, Iago is a masterful deceiver who fools everyone in the play, not just Othello. It can be argued, however, that Othello's jealousy is an irrational eruption or a character flaw that cannot and need not be accounted for rationally. Still, some will think that a man of noble character and one who loves his wife as much as Othello claims to love Desdemona would not condemn his wife on so little evidence.

Words to Own Worksheet, Act III

Developing Vocabulary

Sentences will vary. Sample responses follow. Vocabulary words are shown in italics.

1. Robert must *procure* the documents that he needs in order to apply for his visa.

2. There is an *affinity* between us—we are third cousins.

3. The *penitent* child apologized without being asked to do so.

4. From time to time I would *ruminate* over the cause of the argument.

5. When we read a story, we may make an *inference* about a character because the author has not made all the information explicit.

6. The lawyer attended to the *disposition* of the heiress's estate.

7. Susan was so *vehement* in her denial that we started to believe that she was indeed innocent.

8. The speaker's *tranquil* attitude helped to calm the impatient crowd.

9. I am *compulsive* about working out and so feel guilty when I skip a day.

10. I *loathed* the city and would go there only when absolutely necessary.

Literary Elements Worksheet, Act III

Understanding Conflict

1. Desdemona and Othello; external conflict over the reinstatement of Cassio.

2. Othello; internal conflict over whether to believe Iago's charges against Desdemona and how to react to her suspected adultery.

3. Iago and Othello; external conflict over the truth of Iago's accusations against Desdemona.

4. Othello; internal conflict regarding Desdemona's love and fidelity.

5. Othello; internal conflict between reason and violent irrationality.

6. Othello and Desdemona; external conflict concerning the whereabouts of a precious token of love.

7. Desdemona; internal conflict over the cause of Othello's anger.

8. Cassio and Bianca; external conflict about the significance of Cassio's having a woman's handkerchief.

Applying Skills

Responses will vary. Sample response: The emerging theme is that a man's overweening confidence in his abilities and virtues can result in his own tragic downfall. Othello's tragedy lies in the fact that he is undone by the positive aspects of his character: His overwhelming love for Desdemona

*Drama Study Guide: **The Tragedy of Othello, the Moor of Venice***

makes him susceptible to jealousy, and his mag-nanimous nature leads him to place his confidence in the untrustworthy Iago. Othello is overconfident of his own rationality, mistakenly believing that his passions are under his control, yet he quickly embraces the idea of Desdemona's infidelity even though it is not backed up by experiential evidence.

Reader's Response

Responses will vary.

Test, Act III
Thoughtful Reading

1. d   **2.** b   **3.** a   **4.** c   **5.** c

Expanded Response

6. Responses will vary, but students should support their responses with at least one example from the play. Sample responses are listed below.

   a. This is not the best choice, though a student could argue that *Othello* is a play about love lost—because of Iago's relentless quest to spoil it. A student might point out that once Othello starts to mistrust, or stop loving, Desdemona, "chaos" begins to reign.

   b. This quotation does not adequately express major themes in the play. Although characters worry about their reputations, or "good names," this is not a driving force in the play. Partial credit may be given.

   c. Students may make a good case for choosing this quotation. The play, as a whole, can be read as a statement about the evils of "jealousy." In addition, Othello is blinded by his "love," which adversely affects his performance as a soldier. It is arguable that both jealousy and love are criticized in the play, though a more thorough response might point out that love does not bring about Othello's downfall, while jealousy certainly does.

   d. This quotation expresses the themes of the play better than any other. It expresses the warning Othello cannot hear—until it is too late. Jealousy does "mock" Othello and in effect destroys his life. At this point his failure to hear this message is beginning to threaten his marriage, and his life.

7. The three characters fooled by Iago in Act III are Desdemona, Cassio, and Othello. Because each character is fooled in more than one way,

student responses may vary. Some possible responses are listed below.
Desdemona—Iago persuades Emilia to steal Desdemona's handkerchief, which becomes the false evidence of her infidelity.
Cassio—Iago convinces him to plot secret meetings with Desdemona.
Othello—Iago leads him to believe that Cassio "steals away" because he is guilty of loving Desdemona.

Written Response

8. Responses will vary depending on students' interpretation of Desdemona's behavior. In a model response, students should fulfill the following criteria:

   • demonstrate understanding of the prompt

   • clearly express their interpretations of Desdemona's pleas on behalf of Cassio

   • support their ideas with at least two references to specific details in the play—preferably dialogue spoken, or actions taken, by Desdemona. For example, these are different interpretations of the same event:

      • Desdemona is easily persuaded to conduct secret meetings with Cassio, so it is possible to conclude that she is in love with him.

      • Desdemona is tricked into meeting Cassio, and it is only in the interest of truth and honor that she pleads his case to Othello.

Graphic Organizer for Active Reading, Act IV
Graphic Organizer

Responses will vary. Sample responses follow.

Emilia—worldly; realistic; earthy; skeptical.

Both—loving; loyal; witty; friendly.

Desdemona—naive; idealistic; trusting; patient.

1. Answers will vary. Some students might think that the different personalities of the two women are very important, for they allow the audience opposing views of the same predicament. Emilia's realistic character throws Desdemona's idealistic character into sharp relief. Other students might think that their similarities are more important because it is the qualities that the two women share that make them close friends.

*Drama Study Guide: **The Tragedy of Othello, the Moor of Venice***

2. Answers will vary. Another pair of foils is Iago and Cassio. Cassio is generally cheerful and optimistic about life. He is intelligent, but not clever enough to realize what is happening to him, for he is used to taking people at face value and is not used to deception. Cassio's character is somewhat superficial — what we see is what we get. Iago, on the other hand, is a pessimist and disparages human nature; his intelligence is a calculating, manipulative one.

Making Meanings, Act IV

Reviewing the Text

a. When Othello sees Cassio laughing while talking to Iago, he believes Cassio is talking about Desdemona. When he sees Bianca give Desdemona's handkerchief to Cassio, he is convinced that his wife and Cassio are having an affair.

b. Iago suggests that Othello strangle Desdemona in her bed. Othello responds, "The justice of it pleases" (Scene 1, line 206).

c. Lodovico announces that Othello has been recalled to Venice and that Cassio has been appointed to take his place as governor of Cyprus.

d. Roderigo has given Iago jewels with which to win Desdemona's favor and has seen no results. Iago pacifies Roderigo, and talks him into waiting just one more day for the prize he desires, by flattering him, complimenting his courage in speaking out.

e. Desdemona asks Emilia whether wives frequently betray their husbands and whether Emilia would ever betray Iago.

First Thoughts

1. Responses will vary. Most students will be disappointed with, horrified by, and/or angry with Othello. The man who earlier was disciplined, just, and loving has become violent, irrational, and cruel.

Shaping Interpretations

2. Iago urges, "Work on, / My med'cine, work!" (lines 45–46). He explains to Cassio that Othello, unless left to his "lethargy," "foams at the mouth and by and by / Breaks out to savage madness" (lines 54–56). Othello is indeed beginning to act like a madman: He no longer rationally evaluates Iago's allegations and responds more and more emotionally.

3. In Scene 1, lines 20–21, Othello refers to Desdemona's handkerchief as coming over his memory "As doth the raven o'er the infected house." In line 63, he says in reference to himself, "A hornèd man's a monster and a beast." To Iago, in lines 186–187, he says, "O, she will sing the savageness out of a bear!" As the act proceeds, Othello increasingly uses images of animals in references to others rather than himself. In Scene 1, line 241, he compares a woman's tears to a crocodile's, and then, in line 258, he refers to "goats and monkeys" when speaking to Lodovico. In Scene 2, line 60, he refers to "foul toads" when accusing Desdemona of betraying him. Interpretations of what these images say about Othello's state of mind will vary. The imagery that Othello uses may be an indication that he realizes, if only subconsciously, that unrestrained passions debase humans, making them act like animals.

4. Othello showed self-control when Brabantio accused him of enchanting Desdemona, when he stopped Roderigo and Iago from fighting, and when he was provoked by the sight of Cassio fighting while on guard. When he and Desdemona were reunited in Cyprus, he greeted her with much love. Now he has lost all self-control and seems to have lost all love and respect for his wife.

5. Othello is full of hatred, jealousy, anger, and scorn. He feels pity for himself and admits to a lingering attraction for Desdemona; but convinced now of her guilt, he does not really hear her claims of innocence.

6. The audience knows, but Emilia doesn't, that when Emilia curses the person who has led Othello to turn against Desdemona, she is condemning her own husband. Desdemona, too, is ignorant of what the audience knows: that the man she is turning to for advice is the person responsible for her problem.

7. Emilia is worldly and knows that many husbands and wives betray each other and that husbands often unfairly invoke a double standard when women break their marriage vows. Desdemona, in contrast, is unworldly and idealistic in the extreme, unable even to imagine herself or others being unfaithful. Emilia's morality is relative; she admits that she might betray her husband if the rewards were sufficiently great, whereas Desdemona's commitment to Othello is absolute.

Connecting with the Text

8. Responses will vary. Some students may feel great sympathy for the innocent Desdemona and outrage at the injustice and cruelty of Othello's accusations. Others may feel impa-

tience with Desdemona's passivity. Although innocent, she does not get angry at being falsely accused and fails to protect herself against her husband's wrath.

Extending the Text

9. Responses will vary. An innocent wife might react with anger and indignation or with counter accusations; she might try to reason with her husband and ask him to prove his suspicions; or she might refuse to respond at all to such nonsense. Emilia would have more likely reacted in an active, angry way than in a passive, sad way.

Words to Own Worksheet, Act IV

Developing Vocabulary

Sentences will vary. Sample responses follow. Vocabulary words are shown in italics.

1. We don't see as many people in their *dotage* these days, for medical breakthroughs have made possible a long, healthy life.
2. My younger brother Jamal has a *credulous* nature; he believes everything we tell him.
3. His *lethargy* prevented him from participating in sports or joining a club.
4. The trickster polished his routine as he prepared to *beguile* the next dupe.
5. Each day he *importunes* his teacher to let the class study outside, but she does not yield.
6. The guard was disturbed that we had entered the building without signing in, for this was a *breach* of regulations.
7. A rude answer can *requite* an impolite question.
8. Her son was *impudent,* I thought, for one so young, and he showed no signs of shyness.
9. By always wearing black, Kirk hoped to *shroud* himself in a mysterious aura.
10. The customer was complaining, and his *peevish* behavior was annoying other shoppers.

Literary Elements Worksheet, Act IV

Understanding Atmosphere

Responses will vary. Sample responses follow.

1. Anger; frustration; a sense of impending doom.
2. Apprehension or alarm (lines 179–181); pity, compassion, sympathy, regret (lines 180–188).

3. Fear; alarm; horror.
4. Terror; suspense.
5. Confusion; fear; terror; anger.
6. Wonder; sympathy; apprehension.
7. Assured (of Desdemona's innocence); worried (for her safety); suspense.
8. Sympathy; sorrow; dread.
9. Sympathy; sadness.
10. Respect and admiration (for Desdemona's patient love) (lines 19–22); regret, foreboding (lines 23–25).

Applying Skills

Responses will vary. Sample response: In Act III, Iago manages to convince Othello of Desdemona's infidelity, and the audience grows concerned about her safety. In Act IV, the mood of fear and terror increases. Although Othello's violent behavior in this scene turns the audience against him, there are also moments when we feel sympathy for Othello. For example, his speech in Scene 2, lines 46–63, serves to remind the audience that Othello's anger stems from the same source as his love. Desdemona's confusion and hurt (Scene 1, lines 229 and 236, and the whole of Scene 3) convince the audience that she is innocent; the injustice of the accusation is therefore underscored, and we feel anger as well as sorrow at the probable outcome of events.

Test, Act IV

Thoughtful Reading

1. c   2. b   3. a   4. d   5. a

Expanded Response

6. Responses will vary. Because Othello's emotions are confused and quickly changing at this point in the play, a case can be made for almost any of the four answers. However, some responses can be more persuasively defended than others. Possible defenses for each answer are provided.

   a. Othello is both jealous and full of rage. He doesn't listen to Emilia or Desdemona and prays for his own wife's damnation.

   b. Othello is disillusioned and humiliated, but these are the emotions that have caused this tirade, not the feelings expressed in the scene itself.

   c. Othello is cruel here, and his actions could be described as cold, especially when

*Drama Study Guide: **The Tragedy of Othello, the Moor of Venice***

Desdemona pleads for his affections and expresses her own. However, Othello truly believes that his wife has been unfaithful. His actions are motivated by his anger, not by sheer cruelty.

    d. Othello does feel self-pity, but this description is hardly adequate to describe his full range of emotions. His self-pity is outweighed by his jealousy and his rage.

7. Answers will vary, but for each characteristic, students should provide one example from Acts I-III and one example from Act IV that show the change in his behavior. Othello's behavior has changed so much by Act IV that students will have a variety of examples to choose from. Possible responses are listed below.

Self-confidence—Act I, Scene 2: Othello disputes Brabantio and the senators over his right to marry Desdemona; Act IV: Othello doubts Desdemona's honesty without having any real evidence of her betrayal.

Loving—Act II, Scene 3: Othello chooses to spend the hours of the celebration with Desdemona rather than with his fellow soldiers; Act IV: Othello strikes Desdemona when she expresses pleasure at Cassio's appointment as Othello's successor in Cyprus.

Self-control—Act III, Scene 3: When Desdemona pleads on behalf of Cassio, Othello, though suspicious, agrees to consider her request, waiting for a moment alone to indulge his fears; Act IV: Othello's jealousy sends him into an epileptic trance; he is no longer in control.

Written Response

8. Responses will vary, depending on students' interpretation of Othello's behavior toward Desdemona and Emilia. In a model response, students should fulfill the following criteria:

- demonstrate understanding of the prompt
- clearly express their interpretations of Othello's behavior
- support their ideas with at least two references to specific details in Scene 3. Some possible details are provided.
  - Desdemona still feels compassion for Othello.
  - Othello has been driven mad by jealousy.
  - Othello's suspicions are the result of Iago's insinuations.
  - Othello's temper has become violent.
  - Othello's refusal to listen to Desdemona and Emilia only fuels his rage. He rejects the explanations that could subdue him.

*Drama Study Guide: **The Tragedy of Othello, the Moor of Venice***

Graphic Organizer for Active Reading, Act V

Graphic Organizer

Sample responses are provided.

Rising Action—Act II, Scene 1, when Iago reveals his intention of making Othello jealous, or Act II, Scene 3, when Iago puts his plan into action.

Turning Point—Act III, Scene 3, when Iago convinces Othello of Desdemona's infidelity.

Falling Action—Act IV, Scene 1, when Othello strikes Desdemona, or Act IV, Scene 2, in which the marriage seems to be irreconcilable.

Climax—Act V, Scene 2, when Othello murders Desdemona.

Resolution—Act V, Scene 2, when Othello kills himself.

1. Most students will choose Act V, Scene 2, when Othello, driven mad with jealousy and rage, murders Desdemona. There is no turning back now: Othello has dealt with his conflicting emotions by killing the wife he both loves and fears.

2. Most students will be satisfied with the play's resolution since the two men responsible for Desdemona's death are punished—Iago is taken away by the authorities and Othello takes his own life. Some students might think that it would be more dramatic to have Othello murder Iago onstage. Others might be disturbed that Desdemona, although totally innocent, is dead.

Making Meanings, Act V

Reviewing the Text

a. Roderigo dies, wounded by Cassio and then killed by Iago.

b. Iago pretends to be helping Cassio while wishing him dead. He also pretends to be protecting Cassio while cunningly using the opportunity to kill Roderigo.

c. Emilia exposes Iago's lies. When she does, Othello lunges at Iago, and Iago stabs Emilia and runs off, pursued by Gratiano and Montano.

d. Desdemona claims to have killed herself.

e. Before he kills himself, Othello asks that an honest report of his actions be made in Venice and that he be described as "one that loved not wisely but too well" (Scene 2, line 343).

First Thoughts

1. Responses will vary. Some students will express surprise at the extent of the killing. Some may have expected that Cassio would die, since Iago and Othello both wanted him dead; others may have expected the evil Iago to die so that moral justice would be achieved.

Shaping Interpretations

2. Scene 1 takes place at night on a dark street in Cyprus, where good citizens like Lodovico and Gratiano are afraid to venture. Ironically it is the evil Iago who brings light to the scene. The dark street symbolizes the moral darkness and violence that have taken over the play.

3. Iago wants Cassio dead because alive he would be able to rebut the lies Iago has told Othello about him and Desdemona. He also expresses a hidden envy of the "daily beauty" that Cassio has in his life, which makes Iago look "ugly" (Scene 2, lines 19–20).

4. Iago urges the men to interpret Bianca's facial expression as a sign of her guilt. This strategy of encouraging others to look for truth in appearances is one that Iago has used to his advantage throughout the play, especially with Othello, who took Iago to be honest because he appeared honest.

5. In Othello's speech at the beginning of Act V, Scene 2, Shakespeare uses "light" as a metaphor for two things: Desdemona's life and her virtue. When he says "put out the light," he is referring to killing his wife in order to "restore" her virtue—presumably in heaven. Readers can assume that to Othello, Desdemona may as well be dead as not possess her virtue. According to his way of thinking, she's better off in heaven, where her virtue will be restored.

6. Act V, Scene 2, has many elements that make it a love scene. Though Othello does not yet know that Desdemona is innocent, he now addresses her without rage. It is as if they were beginning to reconcile after quarreling: He kisses her. However, it is too late for them. Othello links love and death in his opening speech, saying ". . . when thou art dead, and I will kill thee, / And love thee after." Othello sees the murder of Desdemona as a chance to renew their love—in heaven.

7. In Scene 2, Emilia continues the contrasting imagery of light and dark, heaven and hell, and honesty and dishonesty in these lines: "O, the more angel she, / And you the blacker devil!" (lines 130–131) and "Thou art rash as fire, to say / That she was false. O, she was heavenly true!" (lines 134–135).

Connecting with the Text

8. Responses will vary. Some students will think that the tragically bereaved Othello takes responsibility for his terrible deed and in taking his own life recovers some of his former moral stature. Others will see him as self-pitying, rationalizing, and worried about his reputation to the very end.

Extending the Text

9. Responses will vary. Some students will feel that today's public, with its taste for tabloid sensationalism, would want to see and hear every detail of such a story of love, jealousy, revenge, murder, and suicide in an interracial marriage.

Words to Own Worksheet, Act V

Developing Vocabulary

Sentences will vary. Sample responses follow. Vocabulary words are shown in italics.

1. The court awarded him a large sum, but full *restitution* was not possible, for the miner's health would never be the same.

2. The outcropping of granite was eerily yet naturally *monumental.*

3. Soda was not able to *quench* my intense thirst; only water would do.

4. The dark and heavy clouds were a *portent* of rain.

5. Many people think that nuclear weapons are *pernicious* and urge politicians to ban their manufacture and use.

6. Romeo and Juliet are perhaps the most well-known *amorous* young couple in literary history.

7. At the snake house at the zoo, Dad pointed out the most deadly *viper.*

8. The acrobat who twists too violently may *wrench* his or her back.

9. The cops *ensnared* the pickpocket by posing as decoys.

10. We were notified that the singer was delayed and that in the *interim* the band would continue to play.

Literary Elements Worksheet, Act V

Understanding Tragedy

Responses will vary. Sample responses follow.

*Drama Study Guide: **The Tragedy of Othello, the Moor of Venice***

1. "O, thou, Othello, thou were once so good. . . ." (Scene 2, line 290); This quote is proof that Othello has fallen from a position of moral prominence.

2. "Fall'n in the practice of a cursèd slave" (Scene 2, line 291); Othello slavishly believes the unscrupulous Iago, an error that causes his downfall.

3. "Of one not easily jealous but, being wrought, / Perplexed in the extreme" (Scene 2, lines 344–345); The character weakness, or tragic flaw, that ruins Othello is explained in these lines.

4. "But why should honor outlive honesty? / Let it go all." (Scene 2, lines 245–246); Othello realizes that his honor, which is dearer to him than his life, is irreversibly lost.

5. ". . . Of one whose hand, / Like the base Judean, threw a pearl away / Richer than all his tribe" (Scene 2, lines 345–347); The wisdom gained at great cost by Othello is that he has destroyed without reason what was most precious to him.

Applying Skills

Responses will vary. Most students will agree that Othello fits the criteria of a tragic hero. Othello's downfall is the result of a tragic flaw or character weakness; he prides himself on his rational capabilities but lets himself be overcome by his passions, thus erring greatly in his judgments of others. Othello also fits the model of the tragic hero because he does gain some self-knowledge and wisdom before his death.

Reader's Response

Responses will vary.

Test, Act V

Thoughtful Reading

1. b   **2.** d   **3.** a   **4.** b   **5.** d

Expanded Response

6. Students' responses will vary. Students should use at least one example from the play but may also use their own attitudes and examples from their lives as evidence to support their choice. Listed below are some possible responses.

   a. Though Othello has lost control of himself and treated Desdemona cruelly, he is in the end a truly tragic hero. He learns his mistake—but not until it is too late.

   b. Though she is not the tragic hero, Desdemona is truly an innocent victim. Through no fault of her own, she suffers the abuses of a jealous husband, eventually losing her life because of Iago's ruthless plot and Othello's weakness.

   c. Though Cassio has been victimized throughout the play, he is vindicated—at least in part—in Act V. He loses his friend Othello, but he inherits a position he truly deserves. Students who sympathize with Cassio will almost certainly do so on the basis of his grief.

   d. Emilia is another innocent bystander who loses her life. All along she has been Desdemona's defender, and she remains so until her death—at the hands of her own husband. Throughout the act, however, she is angry more than hurt or despairing.

7. Students' responses may vary but should resemble these:

   Othello—**d.** remorse.

   Iago—**a.** jealousy; **e.** resignation.

   Desdemona—**b.** despair.

   Emilia—**c.** anger.

Written Response

8. Responses will vary, depending on students' reactions to the deaths of Emilia, Desdemona, and Othello. In a model response, students should fulfill the following criteria:

   • demonstrate understanding of the prompt

   • clearly express their own reactions to one of the three characters' deaths

   • support their opinions with at least two references to specific aspects of the play. Some possible details are listed below.

      • Desdemona's innocence

      • Othello's role as tragic hero

      • Emilia's tireless defense of Desdemona

      • Othello's lack of trust in Desdemona

      • Desdemona and Othello's inability to communicate

Making Meanings, the Play as a Whole

1. All the characters are fooled by Iago's appearance of honesty. Othello is especially confused by the appearances of those closest to him—Iago, Desdemona, and Cassio. Iago explains this difficulty in terms of Othello's character: "The Moor is of a free and open nature / That thinks men honest that but seem to be so" (Act I, Scene 3, lines 391–392). Since Othello's mis-

apprehension causes the destruction of his love and his life, Shakespeare may be saying that it is vital to find the truth behind appearances.

2. The courage, self-discipline, and calm authority that Othello displays early on are undoubtedly related to his military experience. It seems, however, that his experience as a soldier has limited his understanding of the subtleties of emotional relationships: Othello has trouble tolerating doubt. Quickly convinced of Desdemona's guilt, he acts decisively to end his pain and humiliation. Many students will find these reasons sufficient to explain Othello's behavior. Some students may think that a man who is responsible for the fate of so many soldiers should be better able to control his emotions.

3. Responses will vary. Most students will agree that Othello's race is essential. In fact, the subtitle *The Moor of Venice* underscores the importance of Othello's racial identity. The play is built on a number of contrasts, and one of the most important is that between light and dark, which exists on every level—literal, metaphorical, and moral. If Othello were not black, much of the poetry, character development, and dramatic tension would be compromised.

4. Responses will vary. Some students may see no justice or moral resolution in an ending in which Iago remains alive while the sympathetic characters die. Others may point out that Iago is exposed and awaiting punishment. Civil and moral order has been restored by the appointment of Cassio as governor of Cyprus, and Othello, in keeping with the enormity of his crime, has judged himself guilty and administered his own punishment. Many people still desire morally satisfying endings; typically movies show the good guy ultimately rewarded and the bad guy punished.

5. Responses will vary. Students may mention the poems "The Lady of Shalott" by Alfred, Lord Tennyson, "How do I love thee?" by Elizabeth Barrett Browning, and "She Walks in Beauty" by Lord Byron; they may cite *Romeo and Juliet* and the musical based on it, *West Side Story*. Great operas about love include *Tristan and Isolde* by Richard Wagner and *Tosca* by Giacomo Puccini. Films include *Casablanca, Wuthering Heights, Gone with the Wind,* and *The English Patient.* Students may rate *Othello* among the greatest love stories because of its poetry, passion, and extraordinary lovers.

6. Responses will vary. Unlike King Lear and Hamlet, Othello is neither a ruler of, nor the heir to, a kingdom. An audience today would probably identify with Othello because his tragedy is personal. For this reason, Othello's downfall may be very frightening to modern viewers, who can identify easily with his private passions of love and jealousy.

Choices: Building Your Portfolio, the Play as a Whole

Creative Writing

1. Students' responses will vary. Any strong response should be consistent with the play. For example, Desdemona is confused. She does not entirely understand the sequence of events that has brought about her cruel fate. She is also deeply ambivalent about Othello. He has treated her cruelly, but she cannot forget the man he was before Iago's insinuations. In addition, Desdemona is not altogether resistant to death. Her life has become so painful that death might be a relief.

Critical Writing

2. Evidence in the text could support either agreement or disagreement with the quotation. A strong response should take Iago's influence into consideration and defend a position. Some students may feel that Othello is entirely victimized—that Iago's schemes were persuasive enough to convince anyone. Others may feel that Othello is too quick to distrust—that he should have listened to Cassio and Desdemona before condemning them.

Critical Writing

3. Similarities should include the fact that all three are in love with soldiers, all are eager to please the men they love, and all are faithful to their beloved. Differences include the facts that Bianca is the only one to doubt her lover's fidelity, and Emilia can imagine circumstances in which she might break her marriage vows, whereas Desdemona cannot imagine being unfaithful. Desdemona also defends her husband to the very end (even as he murders her), whereas Emilia turns against her husband when she discovers his treachery. Each woman has a different social status, representing the various positions a woman could occupy in Shakespeare's society: aristocrat, commoner, and prostitute. Students' conclusions about Shakespeare's attitude toward women will vary, but most will infer from the varied portraits of these three women that his view was broad, not one-dimensional. Students should support their analysis with quotations from the play.

Drama Study Guide: **The Tragedy of Othello, the Moor of Venice**

Critical Writing

4. Responses will vary, but a strong essay should use examples from the play. Although Othello takes little time to change from an adoring, trusting husband to a jealous destroyer of his beloved, he is unwilling to condemn Desdemona without what seems to him convincing proof of her guilt. Also, it is clear that without Iago's influence, Othello would never have become suspicious of Desdemona. His main fault, therefore, may be that he trusts Iago too much rather than Desdemona too little.

Critical Writing

5. Shakespeare provides a number of motives for Iago's behavior. The most convincing are the ones Iago offers in his soliloquies, when we assume he has no reason to lie. These include hatred of Othello for denying him a promotion in favor of Cassio and a jealous suspicion that he is being laughed at by Othello and Cassio. However, Iago also uses images of the devil, animals, and madness to describe himself and his actions. This suggests a purer, almost un-motivated delight in destruction that is in line with Coleridge's "motiveless malignity."

Art/Dramatic Performance

6. To help students get ideas for a setting and costumes, encourage them to read material on the theatrical history of *Othello*. Direct them to histories of past productions, particularly those with photographs or sketches of cos-tumes and set designs. Discuss whether alter-native set and costume designs reinforce and refresh the underlying themes of the play or trivialize and obscure its essential meaning.

Research/Critical Thinking/Speaking

7. Students can find information about *Hecatom-mithi* in the introductions to many editions of *Othello,* such as the Signet Classic edition, edited by Alvin Kernan. They can also consult works on the sources of Shakespeare's plays. As they do their research, they may want to chart the similarities and differences between Shakespeare and Cinthio on a Venn diagram. When they are preparing their reports, remind them to identify the opinions of the critics they have read and to distinguish these from their own conclusions and evaluations.

Oral Interpretation

8. You may want to assume the role of director and help students choose and perform the scene. Ask students to think about the kind of scene they want to perform—a love scene, an action scene, or a sad scene? Once they have chosen the scene, assigned roles, and dis-cussed their characters, the actors may want to improvise dialogue in order to get a feel for their characters before they begin to memorize and rehearse Shakespeare's dialogue. If a full-scale production is not possible, urge students to give just a dramatic reading.

Critical Writing

9. If at all possible, obtain a video of *Othello* to show in class. The most widely known films are Orson Welles's 1952 version and Stuart Burge's 1965 version, a record of England's National Theater production with Laurence Olivier in the title role. The most recent film, directed by Oliver Parker, was released in 1995 and stars Kenneth Branagh as Iago and Laurence Fishburne as Othello.

Creative Writing

10. Make sure students re-read "The Renaissance Theater" on pages 1–7 of the HRW Classics edition of *Othello*. If students choose to work on the staging of a scene, have them consider setting, costumes, sound effects, and props. Artistic students might sketch or make a model of the scene. If students choose to describe an audience member's experiences, they should include sensory details.

Creative Writing

11. Before students begin writing, have them de-velop the major characters who will appear in their prequel. Suggest that they brainstorm to come up with character traits for each one. The prequel can be written as a short story or as a poem. Students may want to imitate the dra-matic monologue form used by Browning.

Language Link Worksheet

Understanding Shakespeare's Language

1. you; has; yours; should
2. here on *or* now on
3. to; mockery *or* ridicule; you
4. it was; it was
5. Please; your; wait
6. I think; has; never; has acted like a ruffian *or* hoodlum

*Drama Study Guide: **The Tragedy of Othello, the Moor of Venice***

7. here; you are

8. Did you

9. you do; you are; weigh your; you give

10. Fetch it; see it

11. You said; over *or* to; does; over

12. you; are; smell

13. truth; you would

14. tell us; has happened

15. Yes; you dic

Test, the Play as a Whole

Responding to Literature

Responses will vary. Sample responses follow.

1. *Character*—Iago; *Lie*—In Act II, Scene 1, he tells Roderigo that Desdemona is in love with Cassio; *Emotion*—cynical opportunism; *Consequence*—Roderigo is turned against Cassio.

   Character—Emilia; *Lie*—In Act III, Scene 4, she denies knowing where Desdemona's handkerchief is; *Emotion*—uneasy betrayal; *Consequence*—Desdemona, in turn, is forced to lie about the handkerchief.

   Character—Desdemona; *Lie*—In Act III, Scene 4, Desdemona claims that she has not lost the handkerchief; *Emotion*—confused and anxious fear; *Consequence*—Othello is convinced that she is lying not only about the handkerchief but also about her relationship with Cassio.

2. Responses will vary. Sample responses follow.

   a. *Example*—Act II, Scene 3, lines 275–277; *Effect*—Cassio, in ascribing his behavior to hellish forces, contributes to the feeling of uncontrollable fate and impending doom.

   b. *Example*—Act II, Scene 1, lines 292–293; *Effect*—By conveying the idea that the effects of jealousy and envy are as disastrous as those of a poisonous substance, this imagery contributes to the fearful suspense.

   c. *Example*—Act III, Scene 3, lines 90–92; *Effect*—Othello, in equating the loss of love with the world's destruction, contributes to the disturbing mood.

3. Responses will vary. Students should cite specific examples from the play, for example: Iago is lucky that the others do not suspect his guile, that Desdemona drops the handkerchief, and that she does not confess the loss of the handkerchief. Othello's fall is the result of chance in that his honeymoon is interrupted; it is the result of choice in that he reacts to a marital crisis with a soldier's solution.

4. Responses will vary. Desdemona's sin appears especially ugly to Othello in contrast to her pale beauty. Her beauty makes him hesitate, but he believes that it serves as a temptation to others and that in murdering her he is fulfilling a duty and carrying out an act of justice.

Testing the Genre

Understanding Vocabulary

1. c   2. a   3. b   4. d   5. a

Thoughtful Reading

6. b   7. d   8. c   9. a   10. c

Expanded Response

11. Responses will vary. Sample responses follow.

    a. Though Hamlet hates his mother, he seems more intent on reforming her than on breaking their tie (lines 58–64 and 64–70).

    b. The language Hamlet uses to describe Gertrude and Claudius's marriage seems calculated to arouse shame and abhorrence (lines 57–64, 77–80, and 82–87).

    c. Hamlet tells his mother that he wishes to "wring" her heart (line 28).

    d. Hamlet may be using anger to get his mother's attention.

Written Response

12. Responses will vary. In a model response, students should fulfill the following criteria:

    • demonstrate understanding of the prompt

    • clearly state similarities and differences between Hamlet's treatment of his mother and Othello's treatment of Desdemona

    • support their ideas with at least two references to each of the plays. For example:

      • Both men feel and express an intense rage toward someone they love.

      • Both men are under the influence of another character.

      • Othello kills his wife whereas Hamlet spares his mother.

      • Hamlet tells Gertrude the reason for his anger whereas Othello never tells Desdemona the reason for his anger.

*Drama Study Guide: **The Tragedy of Othello, the Moor of Venice***